5/17

Exploring Swift Playgrounds

The Fastest and Most Effective Way to Learn to Code and to Teach Others to Use Your Code

Jesse Feiler

Apress®

Exploring Swift Playgrounds: The Fastest and Most Effective Way to Learn to Code and to Teach Others to Use Your Code

Jesse Feiler
Plattsburgh, New York, USA

ISBN-13 (pbk): 978-1-4842-2646-9   ISBN-13 (electronic): 978-1-4842-2647-6
DOI 10.1007/978-1-4842-2647-6

Library of Congress Control Number: 2017938279

Managing Director: Welmoed Spahr
Editorial Director: Todd Green
Acquisitions Editor: Aaron Black
Development Editor: James Markham
Technical Reviewer: Massimo Nardone
Coordinating Editor: Jessica Vakili
Copy Editor: Corbin Collins
Compositor: SPi Global
Indexer: SPi Global
Artist: SPi Global
Cover image designed by Freepik

Distributed to the book trade worldwide by Springer Science+Business Media New York, 233 Spring Street, 6th Floor, New York, NY 10013. Phone 1-800-SPRINGER, fax (201) 348-4505, e-mail orders-ny@springer-sbm.com, or visit www.springeronline.com. Apress Media, LLC is a California LLC and the sole member (owner) is Springer Science + Business Media Finance Inc (SSBM Finance Inc). SSBM Finance Inc is a **Delaware** corporation.

For information on translations, please e-mail rights@apress.com, or visit http://www.apress.com/rights-permissions.

Apress titles may be purchased in bulk for academic, corporate, or promotional use. eBook versions and licenses are also available for most titles. For more information, reference our Print and eBook Bulk Sales web page at http://www.apress.com/bulk-sales.

Any source code or other supplementary material referenced by the author in this book is available to readers on GitHub via the book's product page, located at www.apress.com/978-1-4842-2646-9. For more detailed information, please visit http://www.apress.com/source-code.

Printed on acid-free paper

Contents at a Glance

Contents

About the Author

Jesse Feiler is a developer, consultant, and author focusing on Apple technologies for small businesses and nonprofit organizations. His projects have included database design and development with FileMaker and Core Data as well as production process control, publishing project management, and social media strategies for clients such as Federal Reserve Bank of New York, Young & Rubicam, Cutter Consortium, and Archipenko Foundation. His books have been published by Wiley, Pearson, Apress, and others. His apps, including Utility Smart, Minutes Machine, Saranac River Trail, and The Nonprofit Risk App, are published by Champlain Arts Corp (http://champlainarts.com). He is founder of Friends of Saranac River Trail, Inc. and has served on a variety of boards for libraries and nonprofit cultural organizations. A native of Washington, DC, he has lived in New York City and currently lives in Plattsburgh, New York. He can be reached at jfeiler@champlainarts.com.

About the Technical Reviewer

Massimo Nardone has more than 22 years of experiences in Security, Web/Mobile development, Cloud and IT Architecture. His true IT passions are Security and Android.

He has been programming and teaching how to program with Android, Perl, PHP, Java, VB, Python, C/C++ and MySQL for more than 20 years.

He holds a Master of Science degree in Computing Science from the University of Salerno, Italy.

He has worked as a Project Manager, Software Engineer, Research Engineer, Chief Security Architect, Information Security Manager, PCI/SCADA Auditor and Senior Lead IT Security/Cloud/SCADA Architect for many years.

Technical skills include: Security, Android, Cloud, Java, MySQL, Drupal, Cobol, Perl, Web and Mobile development, MongoDB, D3, Joomla, Couchbase, C/C++, WebGL, Python, Pro Rails, Django CMS, Jekyll, Scratch, etc.

He currently works as Chief Information Security Office (CISO) for Cargotec Oyj.

He worked as visiting lecturer and supervisor for exercises at the Networking Laboratory of the Helsinki University of Technology (Aalto University). He holds four international patents (PKI, SIP, SAML and Proxy areas).

Massimo has been reviewing more than 40 IT books for different publishing company and he is the coauthor of *Pro Android Games* (Apress, 2015).

This book is dedicated to Antti Jalonen and his family who are always there when I need them.

Introduction

Once you get beyond the basics of very simple code that doesn't do very much, you quickly discover a conundrum: testing code to do something pretty simple in the context of an app requires you to write a pretty complicated app—in many cases before you can test your simple code. Apple's Swift playgrounds address that issue in many of its guises. With a playground, you can experiment with a simple snippet of code on its own or within a playground that provides the context that your snippet will run in. You don't have to write the whole app in order to test your few lines of code.

You can use a Swift playground as a trainer or teacher: you can build the app context as a playground so that your students can write their snippets inside your playground. Because playgrounds are often used for training and documentation, Apple's Swift playgrounds support their own markup language that lets you format your code and create areas of the playground's code where the user can or must provide their own code. You can even hide some of your playground context so that the user or learner sees only the snippet to be worked with.

Swift playgrounds can be built and run with Playgrounds for iPad or with Xcode for macOS. The code that you write in a playground can be tested in that standalone environment and then copied and pasted into an app being developed with Xcode for macOS, iOS, watchOS, or tvOS.

This book provides an introduction to Swift playgrounds and gets you started either as a developer of playgrounds or a user of playgrounds developed by someone else. As the book progresses, you'll see how to build more and more complex playgrounds.

Playgrounds can provide a powerful and intriguing entry into coding for new coders of any age or background.

Downloading Playgrounds for the Book

You can download playgrounds from the book from the author's website at northcountryconsulting.com. Create an account, log in, and use the Downloads section on the left-hand side of the landing page.

CHAPTER 1

■ ■ ■

Introducing Swift Playgrounds

Swift is Apple's new programming language being used by developers inside and outside Apple to create new apps for macOS, iOS, watchOS, and tvOS. Most Apple operating systems and frameworks were written originally in Objective-C, and there are bridges between the two so that you can write new apps in Swift that use the Objective-C frameworks, sometimes without even knowing it. Examples and demos from Apple on http://developer.apple.com and at the Apple Worldwide Developer Conferences (WWDC) and Tech Talks now use Swift.

In and of itself, a new programming language isn't an earth-shaking event. Yes, many people think Swift is a terrific language (count me among them!), but new programming languages have appeared many times over the years since the first programming languages were developed in the 1950s. What *is* revolutionary is the Swift playground. This book provides an introduction to playgrounds and covers how to use them with Swift. (At the moment, Swift is the only language for playgrounds.)

This chapter introduces you to the pieces you'll use to put together apps for the operating systems and frameworks and talks about how they fit together. In different ways, Swift and playgrounds simplify the process, but underneath it all, the components described in this chapter are what make apps run.

■ **Tip** If you've used or even just looked at these components in the past, treat this chapter as a review. Things were changing even before Swift and playgrounds came along. The app development process—particularly the management of apps themselves—has been simplified.

Developer Overview

Getting started as an Apple developer has changed a little in the last few years. What hasn't changed is that apps for the App Store (including the Mac App Store) are *curated*— meaning Apple reviews each app and its descriptive materials. Curation helps to enforce basic standards of app quality and security to enhance consumers' confidence in the

© Jesse Feiler 2017
J. Feiler, *Exploring Swift Playgrounds*, DOI 10.1007/978-1-4842-2647-6_1

Apple and App Store brands. The only way an app can be installed on an Apple device is through the relevant App Store using a special code that App Store reviewers place in each app to guarantee that it has not been changed since the review.

That said, there are now more ways to distribute your apps on a limited basis without going through the App Store. One important way to share your work with others is to build a *playground* for part of your app. You won't be able to build the next killer game or must-have lifestyle app using only a playground, but you'll be able to build small pieces of it to try out your concept and share it with friends. You can also build a playground to provide a proof-of-concept look at what your app will eventually be and do.

The App Store review and curation process require that you be a registered Apple developer. You can find out more about the programs at http://developer.apple.com. Most developers subscribe to the $99 per year membership category, which enables access to the App Store as well as to Developer Technical Support (two incidents per year). There are other development categories for corporations and educational institutions, all described on http://developer.apple.com.

Most of the development tools and documentation are available for free through http://developer.apple.com. You may need to register with a valid email address to gain access, but for the most part, there is no cost. Where there is a cost involved is for anything that you use for testing on the iOS Simulator or on live devices. For many would-be developers, that is when they pay the $99 fee.

In short, there's no cost involved in getting started programming with the Apple environments.

Xcode

Xcode is the integrated development environment (IDE) used to develop apps. It's enormously powerful: in fact, it's used to develop the operating systems themselves. This power means that it may appear daunting to use it to build something small like a Hello World app. As your development projects in Xcode increase in size and complexity, Xcode's power and features come into play for you. By the time you get up to even a small app with a user interface for iOS or macOS, using Xcode is more efficient than writing out code line by line.

This chapter gives only a very high-level overview of the Xcode development process. Don't worry, there are a lot more details as we move into playgrounds.

Building the Single View Application in Xcode

Let's start with an example of building a simple iOS app with Xcode. This is not an Xcode tutorial, but rather just a quick look at the Xcode process. As you move on in this chapter and through the book, you'll see how playgrounds can become part of that process, saving you time and effort along the way.

We're going to look at the Single View Application project that is built into Xcode. You'll see how pieces of it reappear in a Swift playground as you work with code in both the project and the playground:

1. Launch Xcode and choose New ➤ Project.

2. Select Single View Application, as shown in Figure 1-1.

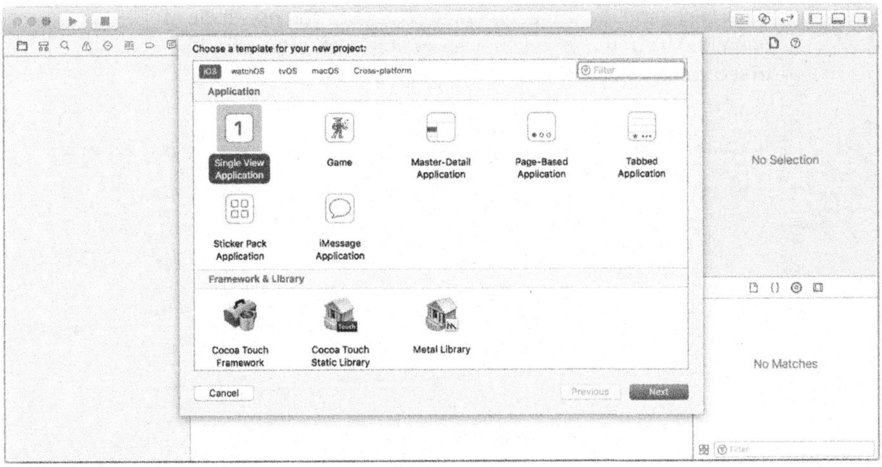

Figure 1-1. *Single View Application has been selected*

3. Click Next and select the options for your project, as shown in Figure 1-2. All that matters right now is the name and that the language is set to Swift.

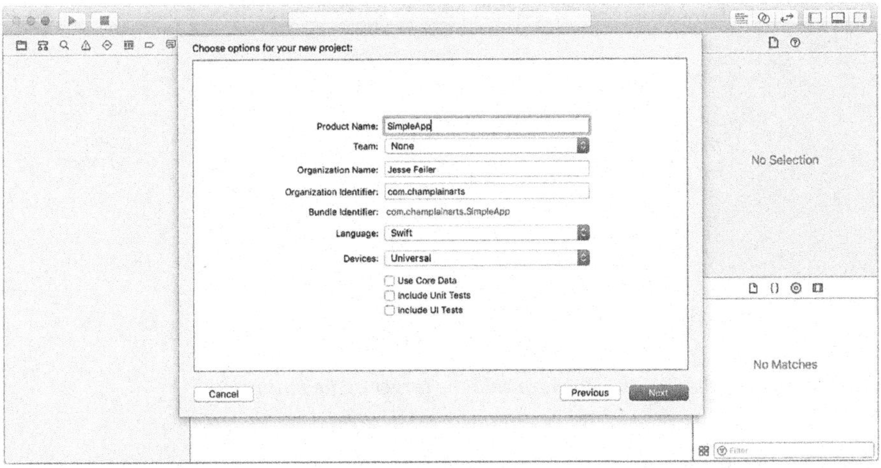

Figure 1-2. *Enter your app's product name and other basic information*

4. Enter a name and location on disk for your project. In this case, the project is named SimpleApp (you can use that name if you want to follow along).

5. Click Next, and the project is created for you. You may have to open folders in the project navigator at the left of the window to see your project files, as you see in Figure 1-3.

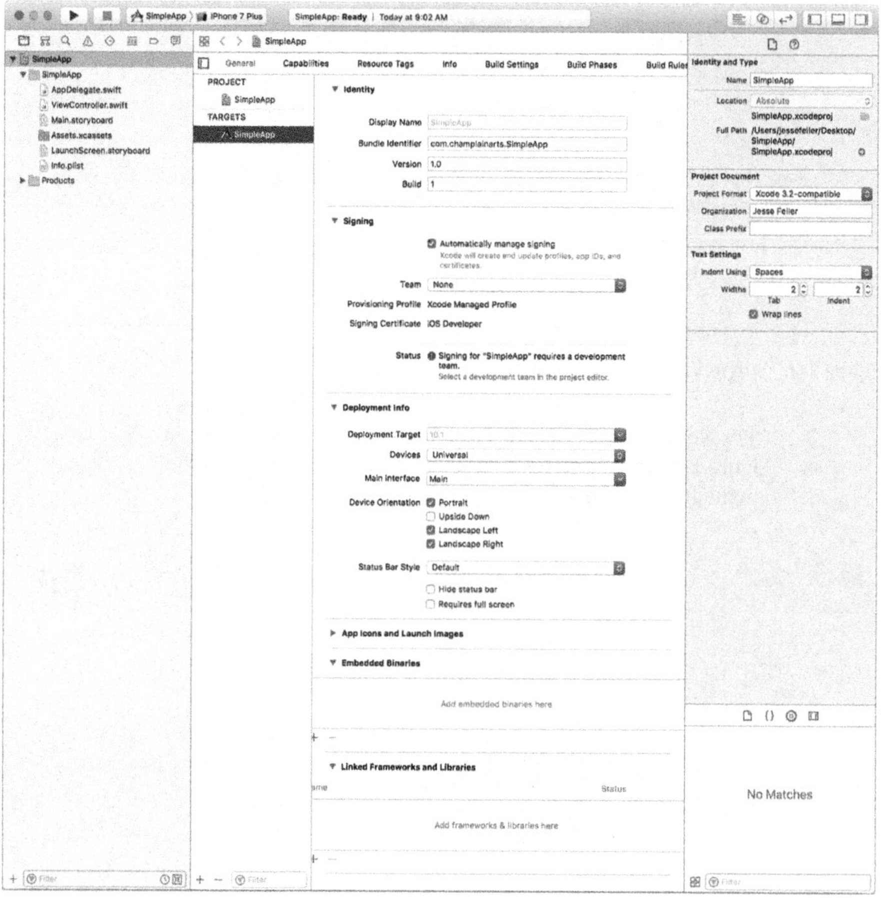

Figure 1-3. *View the project navigator and the target in the main view*

6. Select the SimpleApp project itself (the blue icon at the top of the project navigator). You'll see the default settings, as shown in Figure 1-3.

7. If you see a status warning for code signing, you can safely ignore it for now.

8. Choose a device simulator for the project from the top of the window. iPhone 7 Plus is chosen in Figure 1-3. Click the triangle to build and run the app.

9. The app is built and runs in the iOS Simulator for iPhone 7 Plus, as shown in Figure 1-4. There's not much to see, but the app is running.

Figure 1-4. *A basic app just runs until you create its user interface*

Exploring the Single View Application

You can explore the files that are automatically created for you. They're shown in Figure 1-5. What Xcode gives you is the ability to create all of those files and a runnable app with only a few keystrokes.

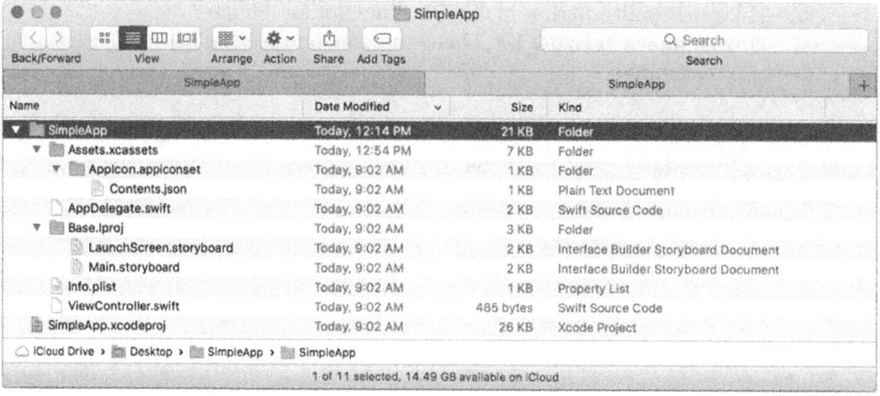

Figure 1-5. *The app's files are created inside the app's folder*

These files are just the tip of the iceberg. If you look inside AppDelegate.swift (one of the main files of the project), you'll see the code shown in Figure 1-6 at the top of the file.

Figure 1-6. *Basic app code is placed in the files for you*

Looking into the Frameworks

Most of the code in Figure 1-6 consists of comments and stubs for functions. At the top of the file, you'll notice a line of Swift code to include the UIKit framework:

```
import UIKit
```

UIKit is the framework that contains the classes to support windows, views, view controllers, and most of the user interface in iOS, tvOS, and watchOS. (AppKit is the comparable framework for macOS). You use UIKit in any app you write that has a user interface, and Xcode puts it in place for you, so you may not even think about it as you develop your app. Other frameworks need to be added for specific functionalities, such as frameworks for system configuration, web services, Core Data, and many more. This integration of frameworks with your code is a key component of Xcode. At the bottom of Figure 1-3 you can see the Xcode interface that lets you add other frameworks.

In short, Xcode provides a simple and almost effortless way of integrating thousands of lines of code in the various frameworks into your app.

Swift Playgrounds

Playgrounds in their basic form won't help you create full-fledged apps. But you can build a functioning playground for testing code and learning how to use the APIs. If you want to build something extremely simple such as the traditional Hello World app that is one line of C code, Xcode and UIKit are overkill.

Building the Classic Hello World App

As a point of reference, the classic Hello World code in C is the following (or some variation):

```
#include <stdio.h>

main( )
{
  printf("hello, world\n");
}
```

(This code is from *Programming in C: A Tutorial* by Brian Kernighan, www.lysator. liu.se/c/bwk-tutor.html).

The heart of the Hello World code is the printf line: the rest is the environment that makes it run. Depending on the spacing, this basic program can be anywhere from one to six lines of code. Certainly, that's simpler than the steps to create even the basic Single View Application in Xcode.

Building a Hello Playground

To build a comparable playground, follow these steps (you may want to compare them with the Xcode steps earlier in this chapter):

1. Launch Xcode and choose New ➤ Playground.

2. Set the options for your playground: the main one is the name. By default, you will probably be using iOS. If that is not the choice for platform, change it. The options are shown in Figure 1-7 (they're much simpler than the full app options shown in Figure 1-2).

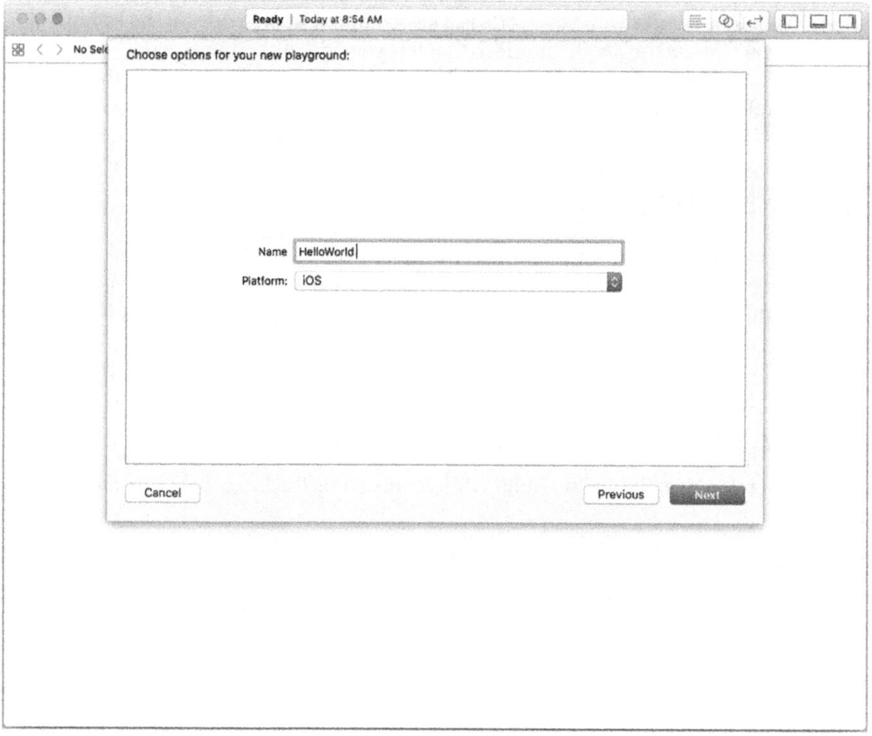

Figure 1-7. *Set options for a playground*

3. Click Next and choose the location on disk for the playground.

4. The playground you created is shown, as you see in Figure 1-8.

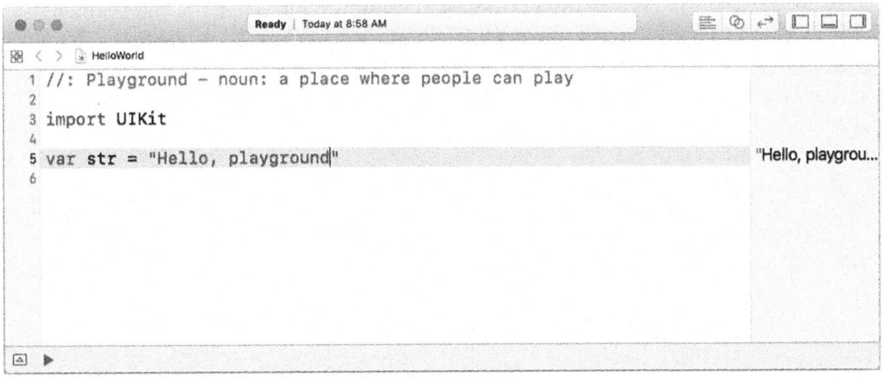

Figure 1-8. *A basic playground is created*

5. You may have to wait a moment for the text in the sidebar to appear. The playground is running, and it needs to make the connection to the interface. Be patient if you don't see it immediately.

6. To convert this to a Hello World app, edit the word playground in the code to world, as shown in Figure 1-9.

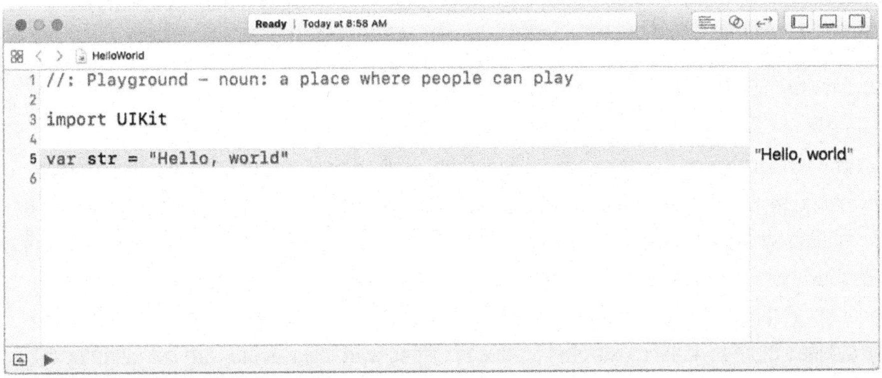

Figure 1-9. *Turn "Hello, playground" into "Hello, world"*

There's no build process, and there's no iOS Simulator—the playground executes in its own window.

Playgrounds and Xcode apps are similar in many respects, but different in many others. You need the overhead, power, and complexity of Xcode to build an app for an iOS device, but you can build code in a playground without any of that. If your objective at the moment is to build and test some code, a playground may be the best choice. Once you have tested your code, you can copy and paste it into an Xcode project.

9

Before leaving this very high-level look at playgrounds, note that the code shown for the playground here contains the default comment generated by Xcode for each playground. It also contains the code to import the UIKit framework. These aren't necessary for your framework, and you can delete them, as shown in Figure 1-10. The playground runs with a single line of code.

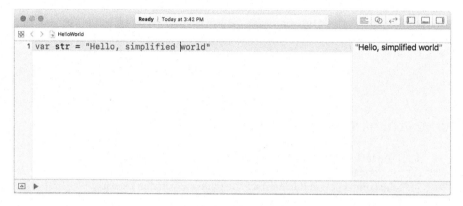

Figure 1-10. *You don't need UIKit for a basic playground*

(Experienced programmers will tell you that deleting comments—unless they are rendered incorrect or misleading by code revisions—is generally a bad idea. This deletion is just to show that it can be one.)

UIKit isn't needed because there are no windows or views. The playground itself displays the result of setting a variable.

■ **Tip**   When we use Xcode or any development environment to test code, we tend to rely on debugging `print` statements. It's an ingrained habit, but it involves writing extra code (and not making syntax errors in the extra code, as well as removing it when it's no longer needed). A slightly more sophisticated technique is to just set breakpoints in the code and examine variables at runtime. With playgrounds, because assignment statements can be echoed in the sidebar, there is nothing extra to be done to inspect variables as they are set. Chapter 4 explains how this can pay off as you move your playgrounds from Mac to an iOS device.

Setting Fonts in Xcode

As you are working with playgrounds, you may want to adjust the fonts both for your own ease of viewing and so that printed or emailed images are easier to read. You can style your default text in Xcode by clicking Xcode ➤ Preferences ➤ Fonts & Colors, as shown in Figure 1-11.

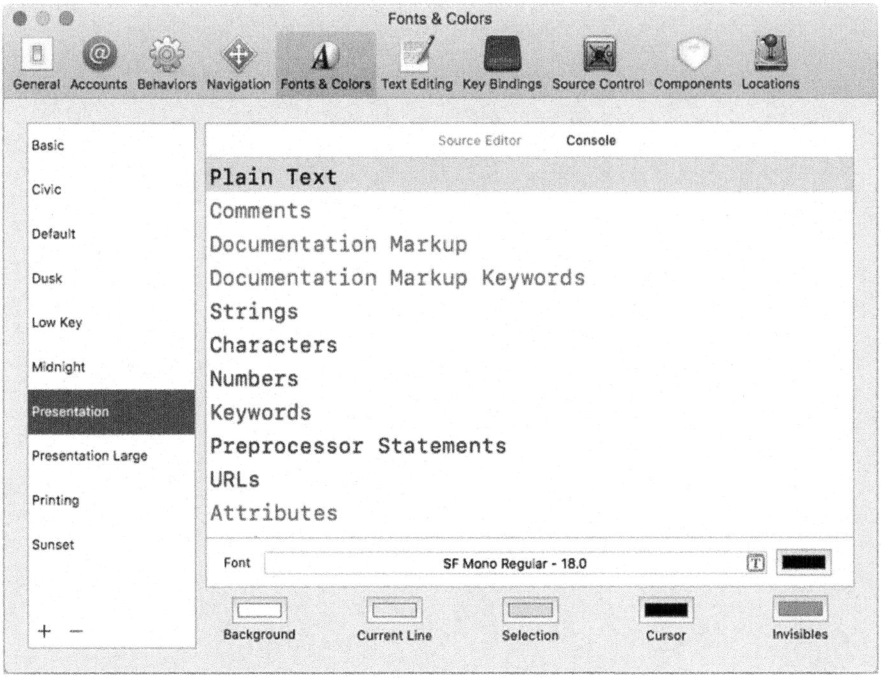

Figure 1-11. *Choose built-in syntax styles or create your own in Xcode's Fonts & Colors panel*

There are at least ten built-in styles for your code. The images in this book typically use Presentation. If you are demonstrating code, you may want to use Presentation Large, which works well on projections. Xcode watches as you type code, so it can color your code based on the syntax you are typing. You can add new styles or modify the existing styles as you see fit.

Summary

Playgrounds are the fastest way to try out code. There is no separate build or compile process because the code is interpreted as you type and you see the results of the syntax scanner as well as variable assignments.

CHAPTER 2

■ ■ ■

Creating a Simple Swift Playground on Xcode

You can create playgrounds with Xcode on macOS or with the Playgrounds app on iPad. The code that you write works in either environment, and you can move it back and forth with a few minor formatting issues. This chapter helps you get started building a playground in Xcode. Remember, a playground is like a sandbox in that it is a safe area to work in without building an entire app. If you're familiar with Xcode, much of this chapter will be familiar, but playgrounds are new to you, and so may be Swift. Or you may have a basic knowledge of Swift and playgrounds thanks to the Playgrounds app on iPad. This chapter can help you get up to speed.

One very important point to mention about this chapter and the following one: the Swift code used is very basic. Specifically, it deliberately uses only the non-class features of Swift. That is to say, this is code that is comparable to code you could write in C or any other basic programming language. Objects and classes (critically important features of Swift and most other modern programming languages) are waiting in the wings, covered in Chapter 4. The focus here is on Xcode and the playground mechanics rather than syntax. There's plenty of that later on in the book.

Getting Started with a Playground, Code, and Results

This section shows you the step-by-step process of writing code, reviewing your results, and printing it out for debugging. In Swift playgrounds, this is similar to other environments, but it's probably a little different than what you may be used to. This section is detailed, but the details won't be repeated in the book each time you use this code and these techniques.

© Jesse Feiler 2017

J. Feiler, *Exploring Swift Playgrounds*, DOI 10.1007/978-1-4842-2647-6_2

Setting Up the Playground

The first example is a playground called BasicPlayground. You create it on on your Mac with Xcode. As a refresher, here are the steps:

1. In Xcode, choose New ➤ Project to open the Options window shown in Figure 2-1.

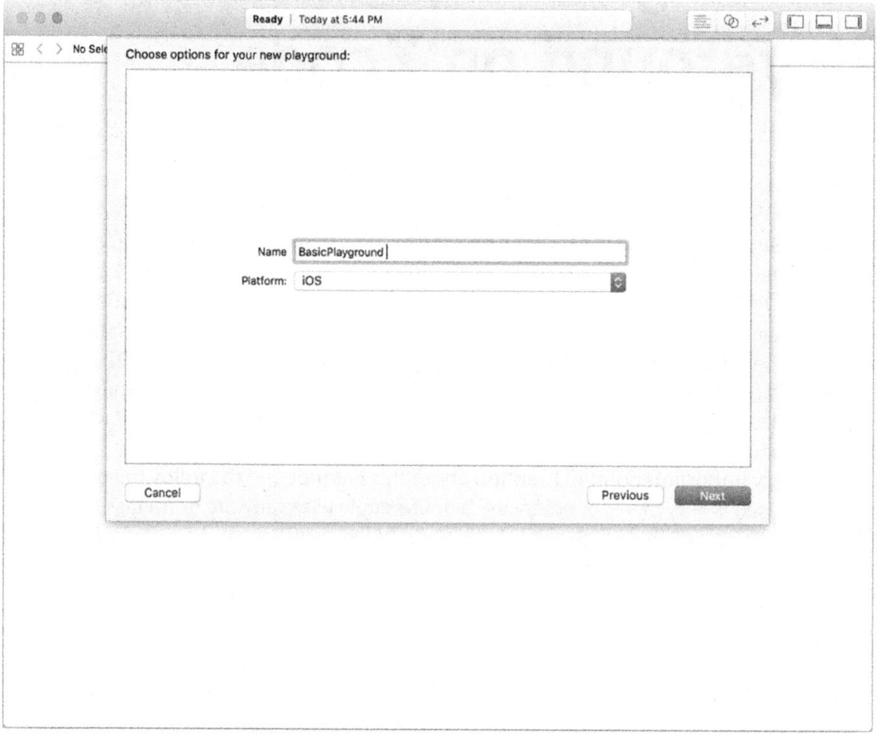

Figure 2-1. *Create a new playground*

2. Name the project and make certain that iOS is set as the platform.

3. Choose the location on disk for your project (note that there will be several files in a folder created for you, so you're only selecting the location for that folder).

You now have a runnable app. When it runs you'll see that the sidebar at the right shows the result of that line of code. In this case, it is the value that is being set for the variable str, as you see in Figure 2-2. You can resize the sidebar as you see fit.

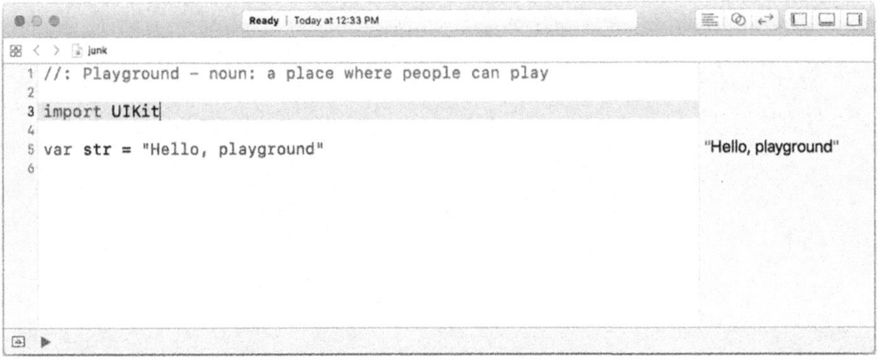

Figure 2-2. *See results in the resizable sidebar at the right*

▪ **Note**   When you first create the playground, you may not see the sidebar log. That may be because the default playground code that's created for you may not show up as anything other than the template. As soon as you actually enter or change code, the sidebar value will be shown. If you don't see it, try just typing in a space or any character and then backspacing to delete it. That will bump the playground into recognizing that you have now modified the code, and the sidebar will be activated.

Watching Variables and Using Code Completion

When you set a variable, its value is shown in the sidebar. Likewise, when you invoke a function or method that returns a value, you'll see that value (there's more on functions and methods in Chapter 4). That's not enough for building apps: you need to be able to display data when you want, regardless of whether it is changed, and in the format you want. Most programming languages provide statements to let you print data in various formats. Swift is no exception.

You can delete the code in your playground window and add a new comment as well as a new line of code that's comparable to the line of code that sets str in the template, as you see in Figure 2-3. A new variable called test is now being set to "Hello", and the sidebar is appropriately updated when that code is executed.

15

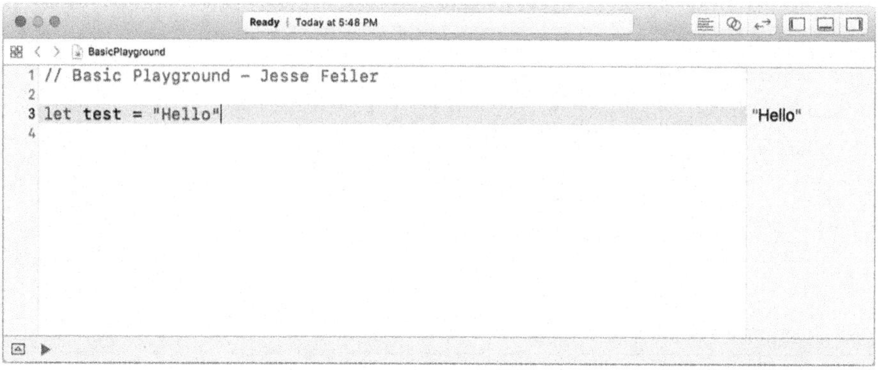

Figure 2-3. *The sidebar updates in real time*

You can print the value of test whenever you want to using the Swift print statement. Don't bother looking up the syntax: just remember (or commit to memory) the fact that the command you need starts with *p* (as in *print*). Add a new line of code and type *p*. You'll see the possible code completion values, as shown in Figure 2-4.

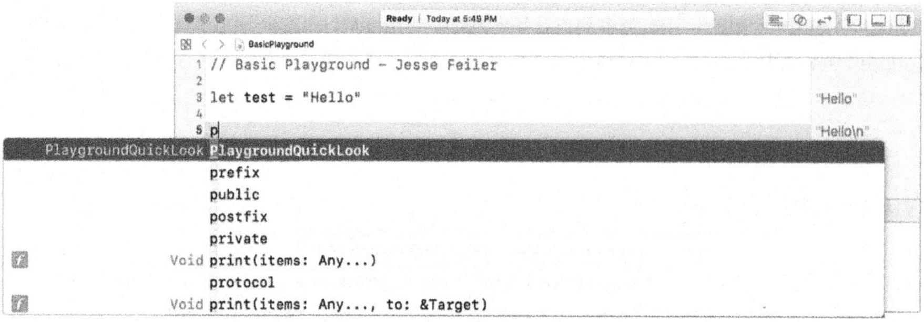

Figure 2-4. *Playgrounds support code completion*

You can keep typing if you want or just scroll down to the code you want to use. Or keep typing by adding an *r*, as you see in Figure 2-5.

Figure 2-5. *You can interact with code completion as you type*

Keep going with the *i*, as you see in Figure 2-6. What you see in this sequence is that the possible choices are narrowed down as you continue to type. At any point you can press Return to accept the code completion, and you can use it as is or modify the code.

Figure 2-6. *You can just type single characters as you go along*

What this sequence doesn't show you is that the possible choices are smart—the playground uses the context you're creating to give you the most likely choices.

Press Return to accept the highlighted code. If you do that as shown in Figure 2-6, the result will be what you see in Figure 2-7. Don't panic.

Figure 2-7. *Sometimes you need to modify the suggestions*

The `print` command has an argument in parentheses—it's shown with a light blue (highlighted) background. In case you can't see it easily in Figure 2-7, here is the code that is in the blue highlight:

```
Items: Any...
```

The light blue highlighting means that you should delete or type over the code from the code completion prompt. If you don't, the placeholder text is interpreted as code, and it generates the error you see in Figure 2-7.

If what you want to print out is the `test` variable, just type *t* over the blue highlight. It will replace the placeholder text, as shown in Figure 2-8.

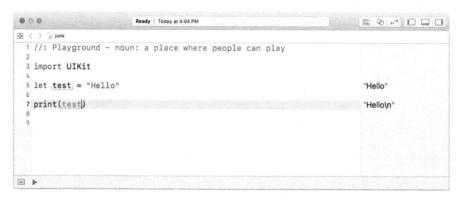

Figure 2-8. *Pick from any syntactically possible completions*

This is an example of the context sensitivity of Xcode: it knows that when you type the *t* into the `print` statement here, chances are you want to print out the `test` variable, but any of the other choices is possible. In this case, just the *t* is enough to construct the correct code, as you see in Figure 2-9.

```
1 //: Playground - noun: a place where people can play
2
3 import UIKit
4
5 let test = "Hello"                                        "Hello"
6
7 print(test)                                               "Hello\n"
8
9
```

Figure 2-9. *Your code is complete*

■ **Tip**   The \n at the end of the sidebar is a newline character—it will print the variable on its own line. In the sidebar, you'll just see the newline character.

There is a debug area that you can show or hide at the bottom of playground windows. Use the up- or down-pointing arrow in the lower left of the window to hide or show it. It is shown in Figure 2-10.

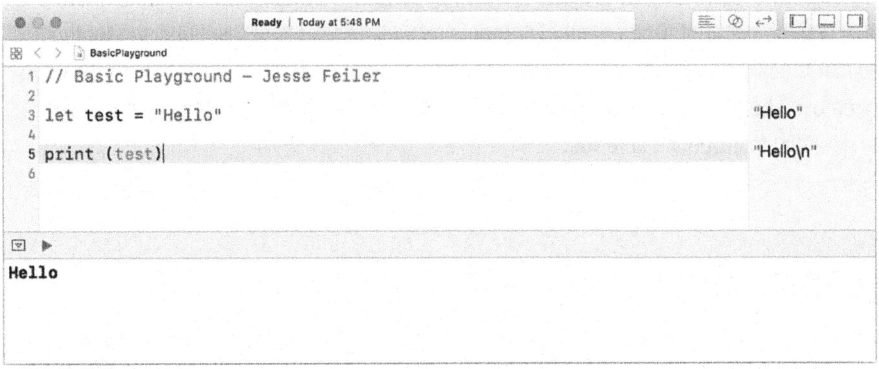

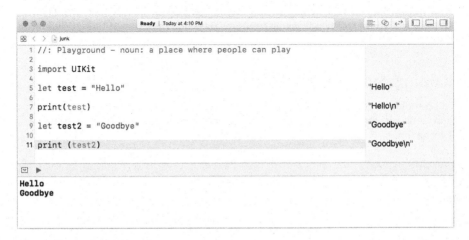

Figure 2-10. *A newline character ends the output line and goes to the next line*

The sidebar shows the formatting code—the quotes indicate what is printed out, and you can see the newline formatting. In the debug area at the bottom of the view, you see the formatted result (no quotation marks, and the newline character takes effect, but you don't see the code).

Add two more lines to the code to set another variable and print it out, as you see in Figure 2-11.

Figure 2-11. *The debug area shows* print *statements but not results of assignments*

What's important to take away is that the sidebar displays results of assignment statements as well as as print statements and the debug area show only `print` statements. (The debug area is also known as the *console*.)

You'll use both of the sidebar and console display over and over.

■ **Tip**   You always see the result of assignment (or the result of a function or method) in the sidebar. If you're used to programming, you may be used to writing debug statements frequently to check that your program is running correctly. Because the playground will show you the result of assignment statements as well as results of functions and methods, you can break the habit of writing those debug statements. Each debug statement needs to be removed before you finish your app. Furthermore, remember that every keystroke has the potential to introduce an error.

Running the Playground

You can control the appearance of the playground and run it yourself. The debug area that is shown automatically at the bottom of Figure 2-11 can be opened and closed with the down-pointing arrow in the box at the left. You can also click the right-pointing arrow to rerun the playground. Try it and you'll see that the debug area is erased and the playground runs again.

Dealing with Errors

There are lots of tools in playgrounds to help you avoid errors and, if they do crop up, to deal with them. The first set of tools is embodied in the code completion technology shown in Figures 2-4 through 2-6. (Remember that code completion includes context sensitivity so that the completion suggestions are relevant to the code you're writing to the extent possible.)

Handling Syntax Errors

Code completion doesn't just come into play as you type new code. For example, in Figure 2-12 you can see what happens if you change `print` to `pring`: you get suggestions for corrections.

■ **Note**   Code completion provides suggestions, but as you see in Figure 2-12, you may also see deprecated code shown with a red line through it. This is particularly helpful if you're working with out-of-date code where, perhaps, code that you wrote a month or so ago no longer will compile.

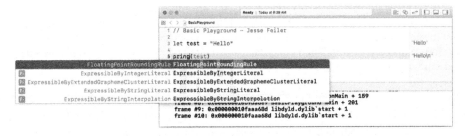

Figure 2-12. *Code suggestions may show deprecated code with a line through it*

In addition to showing you immediate suggestions for code completion and correction, playgrounds in Xcode will give you details of the error in the debug area automatically after a moment if you do nothing. Figure 2-13 shows the actual error message in this case.

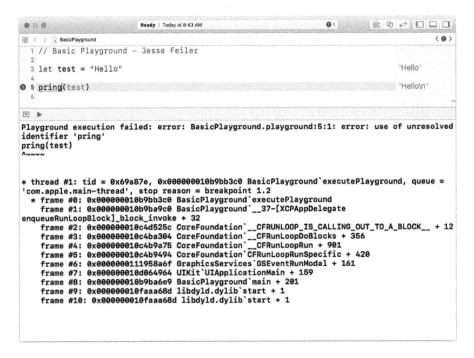

Figure 2-13. *You get full error descriptions in the debug area*

There are several points to think about here. First of all, this is all happening automatically. When you type something that's clearly wrong (`pring`, for example) or begin to type something that you don't complete (`pri` for example), code completion automatically kicks in. After a moment, the playground continues to try to execute, and you see the error. This is happening behind the scenes in the playground—you don't enter a build or compile command.

As is generally the case with syntax errors, the error messages may not be complete. You probably will get information about the code that causes the error shown in Figure 2-13, but the analysis of it may be incomplete or misleading. The best strategy is to resolve any obvious syntax errors and then try and track down more complex problems that may still exist in syntactically correct code.

■ **Tip** As is true in all languages and compilers, the most common source of off-base error messages is unmatched delimiters: parentheses, brackets, or quotes. The absence of a closing delimiter means that the compiler keeps processing what you intend to be code commands as part of the delimited string. When that string reaches a limit, the compiler starts to process your code as a new command. Thus, the error message for a missing delimiter may well be many lines beyond or before the actual error of the missing delimiter. One way to handle this is to pay attention to the automatic code indentation that is generated for you—the code won't line up properly if the delimiters don't match. You can also use Xcode's Fonts & Colors pane in Xcode Preferences (Xcode ➤ Preferences) as a guide. Mismatched delimiters may cause the code colors to be wrong.

Handling Contextual Errors

As in any programming language and environment, some of the errors aren't just misspellings. Code that may appear to be correct may not be correct in a specific context. In Figure 2-14, you can see test misspelled as tst.

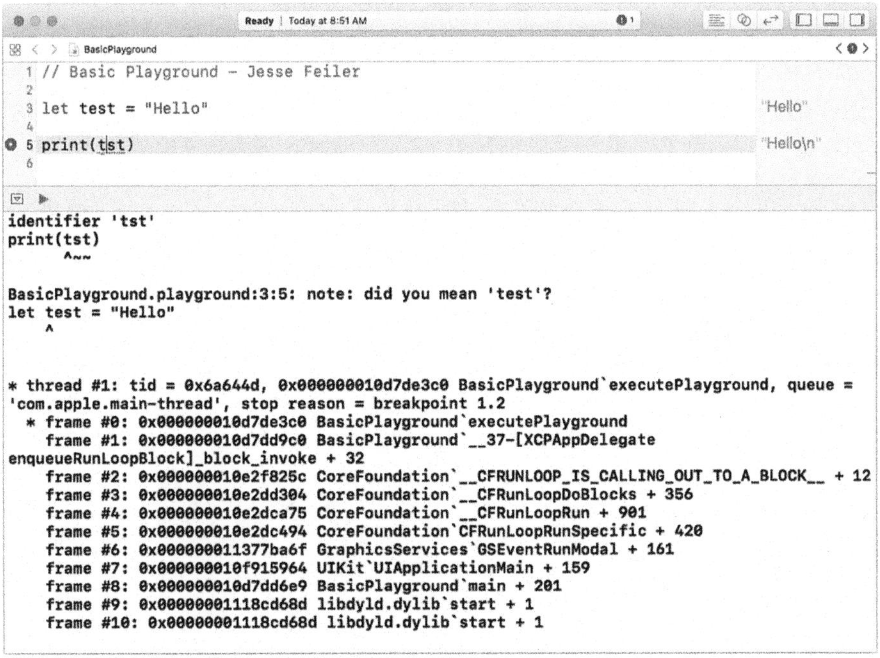

Figure 2-14. tst is a contextual error in in this case

■ **Note**   This is a contextual error because in other contexts, the code `print(tst)` would be correct (if `tst` were a known variable). `pring(anything)` would be an error anywhere because `pring` is not a part of the language. There is some overlap here because `pring` might be a valid function you have created, but the general principle of context vs. syntax applies.

In this case, as in the previous examples, the feedback in the playground is nearly instantaneous because the playground is parsing your code as you type. If you compare Figure 2-13 with Figure 2-14, you'll notice that the red indicator of the error shown in the gutter to the left of the code is different in the two cases. In Figure 2-13, there is a red circle with an exclamation point in it to indicate syntactically incorrect code (`pring`).

In Figure 2-14, the message is different, and the error indicator is a doughnut shape with a white center. In the error messages, the playground identifies this as a possible typing error and asks if you meant `tst` rather than `test`. As is always the case with Xcode, you can click this doughnut shape to get Fix-It suggestions as you see in Figure 2-15. (In some cases, there are multiple Fix-It choices: you can scroll up or down to the one you want and then press Return. Alternatively, click the Fix-It you want.)

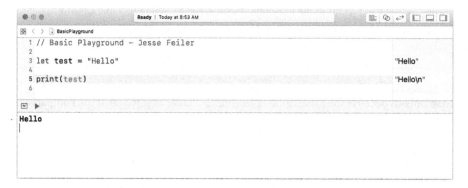

Figure 2-15. Fix-It suggestions offer solutions to code problems

Xcode and the playground will apply the Fix-It, and the playground will run again, as you see in Figure 2-16.

Figure 2-16. The code is corrected, and the Fix-It badge goes away when you click the solution

If you're used to developing code with Xcode or another development environment or with a language other than Swift, you can work pretty much the same way with playgrounds. However, to get the most out of playgrounds, consider relying on the code completion and as-you-type checking so that you can make development and debugging into a single, continuous process rather than type-build-correct, as is the more traditional way.

Summary

In this chapter you saw the fundamentals of coding with Swift in Xcode. Code completion and Fix-It catch possible errors and offer suggestions as you type so that you don't have to type something that may contain an error and come back to correct it when a compiler objects. The immediate response saves time and typing, and, as any teacher or trainer will tell you, immediate response is a great way to learn things.

CHAPTER 3

■ ■ ■

Looking at Swift Basics for Playgrounds

Chapters 1 and 2 cover basic Swift playground features. The Swift code that is shown is very similar to code you have seen and probably written in other programming languages. Although Swift is an object-oriented language, you haven't yet seen Swift object syntax in the first two chapters because the emphasis has been on getting you used to playgrounds and Xcode for entering code.

That changes with this chapter.

This chapter provides a very brief, high-level look at Swift. It's not a definitive language reference (for that, check out the free download from the iBooks Store at `www.apple.com/ibooks/`, with the specific iBook reference at `https://itunes.apple.com/us/book/swift-programming-language/id881256329`). What you will find in this chapter is enough of an overview to get you started reading and writing the Swift you'll need to use with playgrounds. Remember, playgrounds are small and focus on teaching a concept, demonstrating or testing some code to be used in an app, or documenting some code. So you'll not find deep Swift syntax discussions here. If you really want to get deep into Swift and the APIs for Cocoa and Cocoa Touch (for example, an in-depth look at the concurrency across multiple processors that you manage with Grand Central Dispatch), you probably want Xcode and all of Swift.

■ **Note** This overview can give you more familiarity with Swift as you encounter it in playgrounds. If you want to skip over it and come back to it as you encounter these constructs, that's fine.

Comments and Markup

One of the most important features that separates excellent code in any language from other code is the presence of accurate documentation. This ranges from organizational items such as the date and author of the code as well as a description of what it does all the way to well-formatted documentation for the code's users. (Remember that users of code are typically other developers: users of apps are real people.)

© Jesse Feiler 2017
J. Feiler, *Exploring Swift Playgrounds*, DOI 10.1007/978-1-4842-2647-6_3

The basic Swift playground template starts out with a comment that is generated for you automatically. Typically, it looks like this:

```
//: Playground - noun: a place where people can play
```

The comment begins with two slashes, which is typical syntax for a line of comment in many languages. The parser or compiler ignores everything after the comment until the end of the line. For multi-line comments, in many languages you can use delimiters /* and */ to mark the beginning and end of the comment—that is, the syntax not to be parsed or compiled. Here is the same code shown as a multi-line comment:

```
/*
Playground -
noun: a place where people can play
*/
```

Playgrounds and Xcode use rich markup, which adds a colon to the start of a multi-line comment, as you see in Figure 3-1.

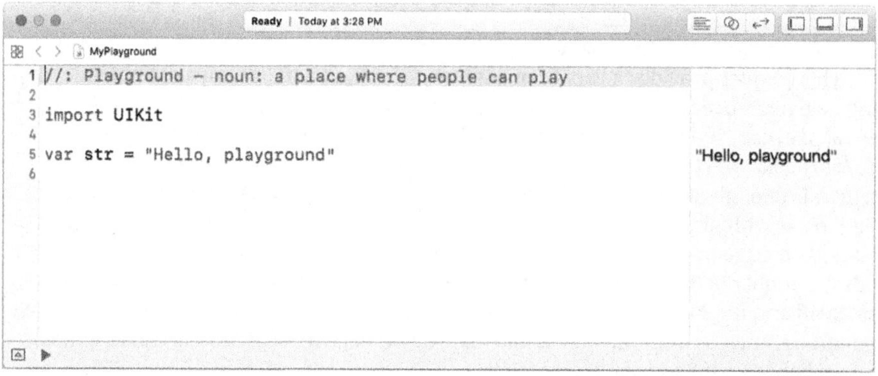

Figure 3-1. Use rich markup with Swift playgrounds

You can use Editor ➤ Show Rendered Markup to render the rich markup, as shown in Figure 3-2, which shows the code from Figure 3-1 rendered. The command switches to Editor ➤ Show Raw Markup so you can use it to edit the underlying text.

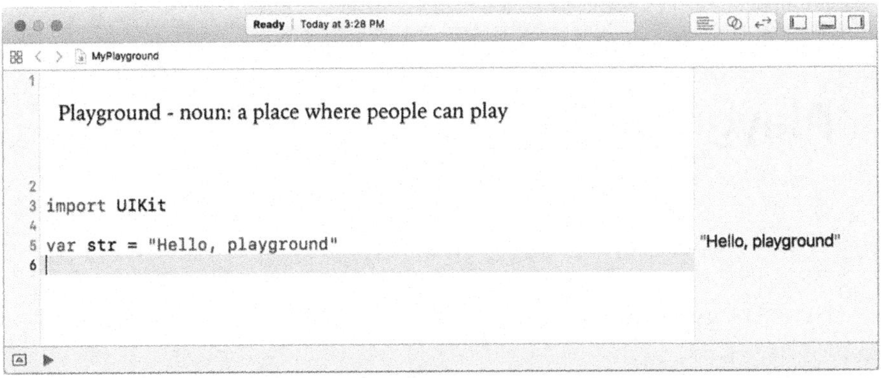

Figure 3-2. *Render the markup with a playground*

You can use more rich markup commands within the // : multi-line comment. For example, Figure 3-3 shows a title style for the word Playground, using a # at the beginning of the line and a bulleted style for the definition using a * at the beginning of the line.

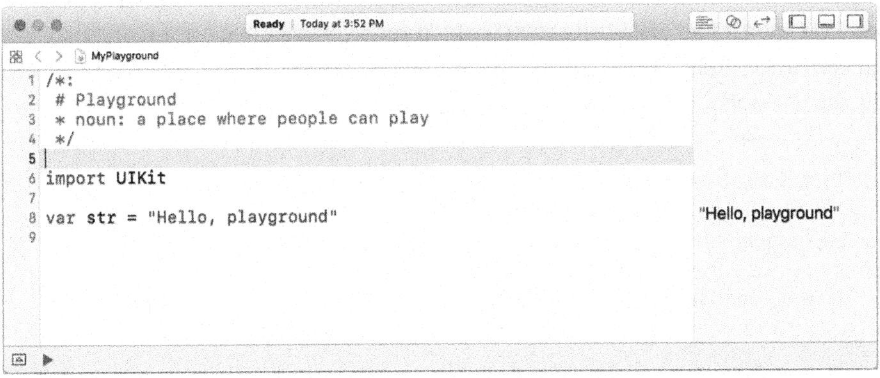

Figure 3-3. *Use headings in raw markup*

The rich markup from Figure 3-3 is shown in Figure 3-4 with Editor ➤ Show Rendered Markup.

Figure 3-4. Rendered markup shows headings and bullets

■ **Note**   Rich markup for Swift is based on Markdown, John Gruber's text-to-HTML tool for documentation. You can find out more about Markdown at `https://daringfireball.net/projects/markdown/`. Apple's rich markup syntax is available at `https://developer.apple.com/library/content/documentation/Xcode/Reference/xcode_markup_formatting_ref/MarkupFunctionality.html#//apple_ref/doc/uid/TP40016497-CH54-SW1`. Note that this includes syntax for Quick Help as well as playgrounds.

Rich markup can make your playground code look much better. In fact, it looks so much better that you can justify to yourself or your boss the time and effort to provide good documentation for your playgrounds. (The time and effort are really not great, particularly when you consider the result.)

Now it's on to the Swift overview.

Globals and Objects

The Swift code and playgrounds that you've seen so far have all been non-object-oriented globals: they are available throughout your playground. In general, globals are frowned upon in modern programming. In object-oriented programming, almost everything is written as an object, so global functions or variables aren't used much.

However, you can declare global variables or functions as well as other Swift syntax. Typically, these are used for special cases (such as perhaps a debugging function that formats data).

Classes, Enumerations, and Structures

Over time, as objects and object-oriented programming have become more commonplace, many object-type functionalities have moved into other programming constructs. With Swift, you'll see overlap among classes, structures, and enumerations.

The heart of your Swift app or playground will be its objects (it is, after all, an object-oriented language). As with most programming languages, Swift objects are runtime instantiations of classes. That is, you write the code for a class, and at runtime it's turned into an object that is executed. If you look at diagnostics, you'll be able to see the memory location for the instantiated object.

Classes may contain *methods* (functions that are placed within the class) and *properties*. Thus, a typical object-oriented class encapsulates the functionality (methods) of an object and the data (properties) that an instance of the class can operate on. Properties can be defined to be part of *instances* (that is, each instance of a class can have its own values for the properties), but they also can be defined as values for the class itself. Thus, for class properties, every instance of the class shares the class properties. Most of the time, you'll work with properties of instances rather than class properties.

You can define a *subclass* of a class. A subclass inherits the methods and properties of its ancestor. An instance of the class Building might contain the property address. A subclass of Building might be House. An instance of House would contain the property address (inherited from Building) as well as its own property, such as numberOfResidents. numberOfResidents would apply only to the Home subclass. A Store subclass might contain a businessName property.

The naming of classes and properties in Swift is enforced by Xcode and playgrounds. Classes are capitalized, and properties are lowercased. Because playgrounds enforce these conventions, you don't have to remember them: you'll be reminded.

■ **Tip** Playgrounds use the capitalization conventions as part of the code completion suggestions so that it knows what you are dealing with.

Structures in Swift play a bigger role than they do in some other programming languages. Classes in Swift are actually structures but they have some additional functions. (Put another way, structures do not have some class features.)

Enumerations in Swift are constructs like classes and structures. If you're used to thinking of enumerations as just a shortcut for integers, you'll see that Swift goes far beyond that.

Table 3-1 shows the major features of classes, structures, and enumerations and indicates which ones are supported in the three constructs. The functionalities shown in the table are generally standard object-oriented functionalities, but there are a few points to bear in mind:

- Classes, structures, and enumerations have significant similarities in Swift.

- Properties in Swift can be *static* (set at initialization or runtime) or *computed* (calculated as needed). *Property* is the term used in object-oriented programming in preference to *variable* or *field*. In database and other general computing terminology, *attribute* is used in a somewhat similar way.

31

- The construct (class, structure, or enumeration) can automatically be initialized with code that you write.

- Swift extensions can add functionality to constructs without modifying the code. Thus, they can be used to extend constructs you don't have the code for.

- Functions that are part of classes, structures, or enumerations are called *methods*.

Table 3-1. *Comparison of Functionalities for Classes, Structures, and Enumerations*

Functionality	Class	Structure	Enumeration
Methods	X	X	X
Properties	X	X	X (computed only)
Initializers	X	X	X
Protocols	X	X	X
Extensions	X	X	X
Deinitializers	X		
Inheritance	X		
Multiple references (access by reference rather than copy)	X		

In terms of syntax, the names of classes, structures, and enumerations that you create are capitalized. Instances of classes, values for enumerations, and properties for all of the constructs use lowercase names.

Types in Swift

Swift is a type-safe language. Many languages (particularly scripting languages such as JavaScript and PHP) take data as it comes and convert it where necessary. In Swift, you have to choose a type for each property you define. However, with *type inference*, Swift often takes care of that for you.

Explicit typing is done with a *type annotation*, as in the following part of a property declaration that annotates age as of type Int:

```
age: Int
```

This would be appropriate for declaring an integer value for a person's age. For a non-integer (floating-point) value, the comparable declaration would be the following:

```
age: Double
```

The annotation is the colon and the type name.

■ **Tip**   `Double` is the preferred type for floating-point numbers. It provides the most flexible data storage. The `Float` type is used in special cases.

You often don't need to set a type for a property because Swift wants properties to have initial value (except in special cases—see the section "Optional Properties" later in this chapter). This means that you can declare a property and give it an initial value, as in the following:

```
age = 21
```

This declares the age property and sets it to an initial value of 21. The type of age is then inferred to be `Int`.

You can use a type annotation to bypass type inference:

```
age: Double = 21
```

Instead of inferring age to be an `Int`, this annotation explicitly sets it to be a `Double`.

You can make the process even simpler for yourself by setting the initial value to the type you want to use. The following two lines of code are arithmetically the same, but the first sets an `Int` value and the second sets a `Double` value.

```
age = 21
aAge = 21.0
```

This is important to remember because if you just look at the code without thinking about Swift types, you won't notice the difference. Watch (and use!) decimal points in setting values in Swift if you want to use the floating-point `Double` type.

There is much more in the Swift documentation as well as in the Fix-It and code completion hints in your playgrounds.

Properties

Swift properties are declared with variations on the following basic syntax:

```
let myProperty = something
```

or

```
var myVariableProperty = something
```

Constants and Variables

You declare a property either as a constant or a variable. A constant (as in any programming language) cannot be changed. A variable can be changed. The syntax is comparable:

```
let birthYear = 1990 // constant
var age = 27 //variable
```

Variables are more flexible, but constants are much more efficient to use because the system knows that once they are set, they can never change. This has benefits in optimizing memory usage.

Whether constants or variables, properties in Swift almost always have values. This comes about in part from experience with other languages (particularly Objective-C), where properties can have values but also can have no values. It turns out that not being able to distinguish between a property that is not set and one that is set to an indeterminate value can be the source of many, many crashes and debugging nightmares. Thus, in Swift, we can assume that every property has a value with two exceptions.

Lazy Initialization

var properties can be declared to have lazy initialization with syntax such as this:

```
lazy var = some expression
```

In these cases, the initialization is done the first time the property is needed. This is a particularly useful optimization in declaring properties that may never be needed—particularly if their initialization process may be expensive.

Optional Properties

Properties can be declared as optional using syntax such as the following:

```
var birthYear: Int?
```

This violates the rule that every property must have a value; however, by declaring birthYear as an optional Int (that's the question mark), it need not have a value. As you see in Figure 3-5, although the property is an optional and is initially set by default to nil, it can be set to a value.

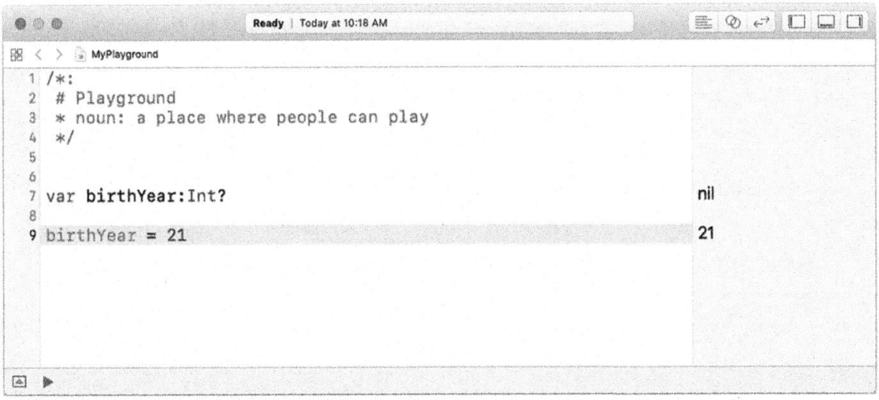

```
 1  /*:
 2  # Playground
 3  * noun: a place where people can play
 4  */
 5
 6
 7  var birthYear:Int?                                      nil
 8
 9  birthYear = 21                                          21
```

Figure 3-5. *Set an optional to a value*

If you print it out as shown in Figure 3-6, you'll see that it is shown as an optional.

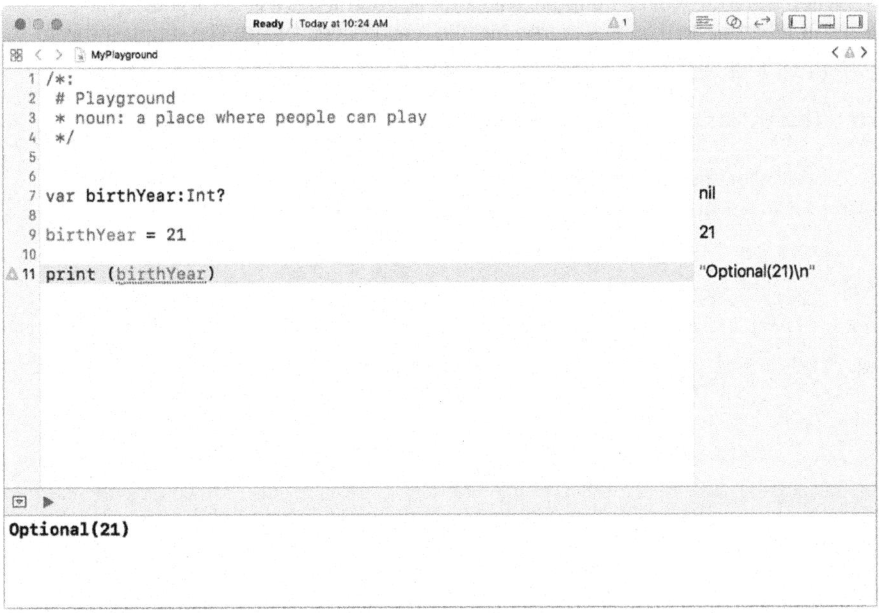

```
 1  /*:
 2  # Playground
 3  * noun: a place where people can play
 4  */
 5
 6
 7  var birthYear:Int?                                      nil
 8
 9  birthYear = 21                                          21
10
11  print (birthYear)                                       "Optional(21)\n"
```

Optional(21)

Figure 3-6. *Optionals are identified as such in the sidebar*

The yellow triangle is a warning, and if you click it you'll see the problem and three potential Fix-It solutions, as shown in Figure 3-7.

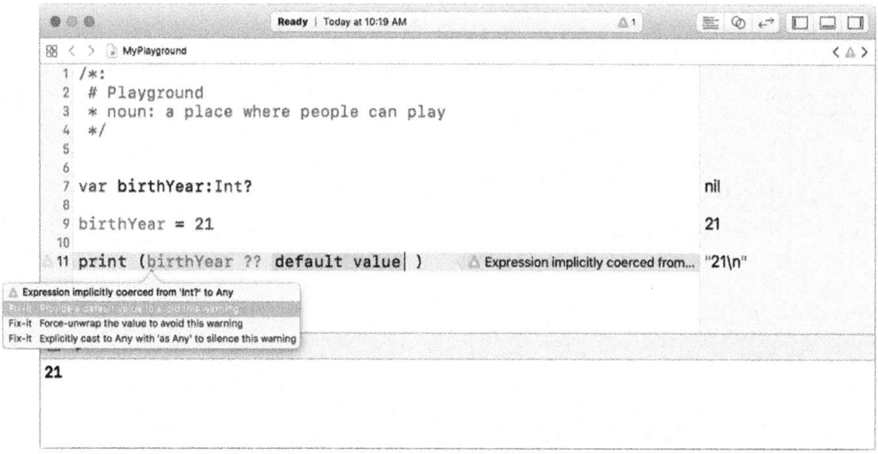

Figure 3-7. *Click the yellow warning badge to see what's wrong*

When working with an optional, checking whether it has a value is your responsibiilty. You do that by *unwrapping* it in one of several ways. The simplest way to unwrap an optional is to use an exclamation point, as in this code:

```
print (birthYear!)
```

The result is shown in Figure 3-8. Note that the value is shown as 21: the ! force-unwraps it so it is now an Int rather than an Int?—an optional.

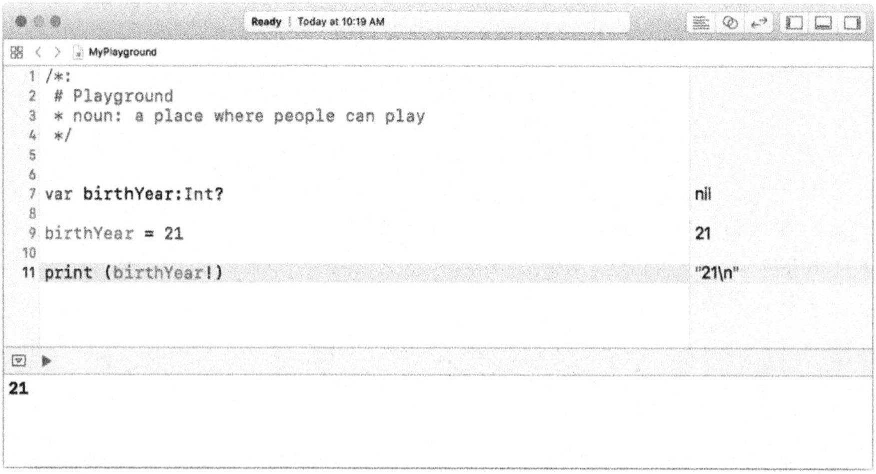

Figure 3-8. *Force-unwrap an optional with* !

If you haven't set the optional, it has no value, so when you force-unwrap it you'll get an error, as you see in Figure 3-9.

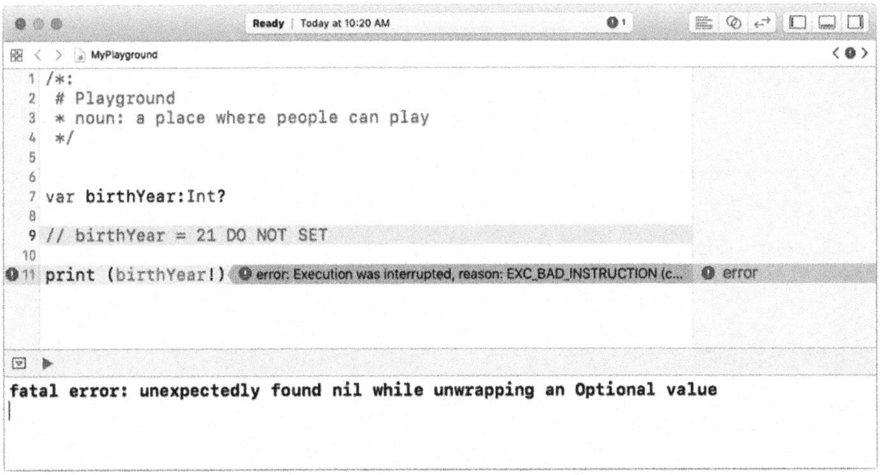

Figure 3-9. Force-unwrapping an optional that isn't set generates an error

One solution to this is to test to see whether the optional is not nil before unwrapping it, as in the following code, shown also in Figure 3-10. That figure shows what happens if the optional remains unset (that is, it is still nil when you force unwrap it with an exclamation point !).

```
If birthYear != nil {
  Print (birthYear!)
}
```

Figure 3-10 also demonstrates an additional technique you can use. Instead of testing to see if the property is not nil, you can use what is called *optional binding* to set a new property to the unwrapped property. That's what the second if statement in the previous figure does.

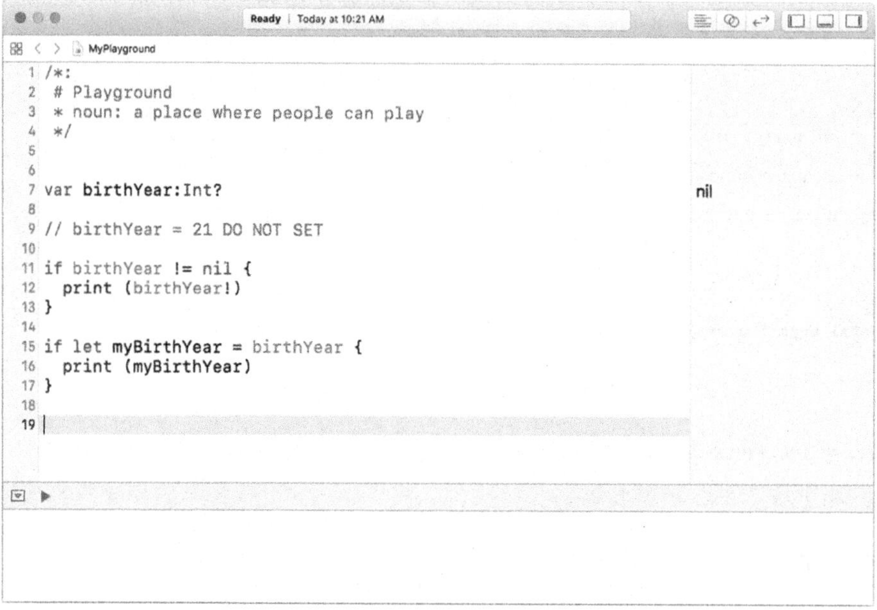

```
1 /*:
2 # Playground
3 * noun: a place where people can play
4 */
5
6
7 var birthYear:Int?                                    nil
8
9 // birthYear = 21 DO NOT SET
10
11 if birthYear != nil {
12   print (birthYear!)
13 }
14
15 if let myBirthYear = birthYear {
16   print (myBirthYear)
17 }
18
19 |
```

Figure 3-10. Work with optionals

The heart of that statement is this line of code:

```
let myBirthYear = birthYear
```

On its own, that line of code would create a new constant (notice let) that uses type inference to be set to an optional of type Int? (the value of birthYear). If you use that clause in an if statement, the clause is evaluated as a Boolean. If unwrapping of birthYear reveals a nil, then the Boolean result is false.

Thus, the print statement is executing using the new myBirthYear constant that is created in the optional binding. Note that you can take an optional variable and unwrap it into a constant in this way. (The scope of the optionally bound variable is just the if statement—it's not valid beyond that.)

Just to double-check, you can test the case in which birthYear is set, as you see in Figure 3-11. Thus, this code works for both nil and non-nil cases. You'll see this over and over again in Swift. It gets around many, many crashes that occur when nil values are set but not caught in other programming languages.

```
  ●  ○  ○                    Ready | Today at 10:21 AM                    ≣  ⊘  ↩   ▢  ▭  ▢
  ⊞  <  >  📄 MyPlayground
   1  /*:
   2  # Playground
   3  * noun: a place where people can play
   4  */
   5
   6
   7  var birthYear:Int?                                              nil
   8
   9  birthYear = 21                                                  21
  10
  11  if birthYear != nil {
  12    print (birthYear!)                                          "21\n"
  13  }
  14
  15  if let myBirthYear = birthYear {
  16    print (myBirthYear)                                         "21\n"
  17  }
  18
  19
  ▾  ▶
  21
  21
```

Figure 3-11. *Work with optionals that do have a value*

These are just a few Swift basics, and they point out some of the differences you may encounter between languages you know and Swift. In the chapters that follow, you'll see Swift used with playgrounds.

Summary

This chapter has covered some of the similarities between Swift and other object-oriented languages, as well as some of the differences. You have also seen the very important aspect of handling nonexistent data using optionals, force-unwrapping, and optional binding.

■ ■ ■

CHAPTER 4

Editing Playgrounds on macOS

There are three basic ways to use playgrounds:

- You can build an ad hoc playground to experiment with code and syntax. Developers frequently do this to test out an idea before incorporating it in an actual project. Particularly if you are transitioning to Swift from other languages (or to Swift 3 from previous versions), it's often faster to test out some syntax in a playground than to search the various versions of documentation.

- You can use a playground that's built as a learning experience by others.

- You can build a playground that serves as a learning experience for others. In a similar vein, you can build a playground that serves as documentation for code you have built or intend to build. (Playgrounds are found frequently as companions to macOS or iOS projects both on open source repositories such as GitHub and on private repositories.)

The first three chapters have looked primarily at the first of these ways to use playgrounds (for ad hoc experimentation). You can use Apple's downloadable playgrounds on Everyone Can Code (`www.apple.com/education/everyone-can-code/`) for yourself, your students, and others.

This chapter looks at building playgrounds on macOS so that they can be used by others on macOS and on iOS.

Exploring the Two Playground Environments

There are two environments for creating and using playgrounds: macOS and iOS. You can create a new playground on macOS using Xcode, and you can also create a new playground on an iPad with the Playgrounds app.

Once you have created a playground in either environment, you can run it on iOS using the built-in Playgrounds app for iPad or you can run it in Xcode on macOS.

© Jesse Feiler 2017

J. Feiler, *Exploring Swift Playgrounds*, DOI 10.1007/978-1-4842-2647-6_4

It's important to note that these two environments are not identical. They are similar in many ways, but there are some differences. The most common way of integrating them is to develop playgrounds using Xcode on macOS and then distribute and run them with Playgrounds on iOS with an iPad. This works well for developing and distributing training materials particularly because the more complex and expensive development environment for macOS is leveraged to be deployed on much simpler and less expensive devices such as the iPad models.

To get started, we'll do a walk-through of the two environments and how they work together in this common scenario. There are three basic steps to follow:

1. Create a playground with Xcode on macOS.

2. Move the playground to an iPad.

3. Run and modify the playground on an iPad.

Creating a Playground with Xcode on macOS

Xcode is the integrated development environment (IDE) for all things Apple software. Apps for iOS, macOS, tvOS, and watchOS are all built with Xcode, which is a free download from http://developer.apple.com. If you're used to writing code, it's either a tool you already know or one that you can learn with relatively little effort (learning the APIs takes a bit more effort . . .).

If you're not used to writing code, Xcode may be a hurdle for you, but it really is one that you need to get over whether you're writing a playground now or something else next year. However, with that said, if you really, really don't want to use Xcode, you can write your code using another editor (BBEdit is a widely used tool). In fact, you could probably write your playground's code using Microsoft Word: you would just save it as a plain text file and copy and paste it into an Xcode file.

That's certainly not at all recommended, but it is possible. The fact of the matter, however, is that if you want to build a playground on macOS, you are going to be writing code, so download a copy of Xcode and install it to begin.

▪ **Note** The only time when an alternate route might be needed is if you really want to get started and can't download or install Xcode right away. This can happen in some places where the computer environments are tightly controlled and permission is needed from a manager to download and install new software. With required signatures and everybody's vacation time factored in, it might take a week or more to actually get a free copy of Xcode installed. In a case such as that, you can start typing code—but get it into Xcode at the first possible moment.

In Chapter 3, the section "Comments and Markup" introduced the basics of markup that you can easily add to your playgrounds to create attention-getting titles that help you structure a playground. You can go beyond that to turn your nicely formatted playground into an interactive playground for yourself and others. This section brings you up to speed on building a basic interactive playground.

Turning a Static Playground into an Interactive Playground

As you saw in Chapter 3, you use rich markup commands within the /*: multi-line comment that ends with */, as shown in Figures 4-1 and 4-2. The raw markup is shown in Figure 4-1.

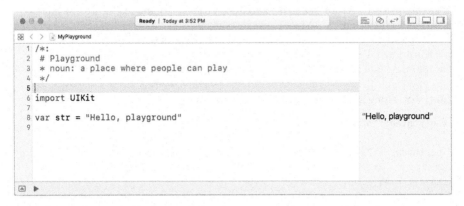

Figure 4-1. *Raw markup for a playground*

In a playground you use Editor ➤ Show Rendered Markup to view the markup when you run the playground.

Figure 4-2. *Rendered markup for a playground*

These examples from Chapter 3 show the basic steps of integrating markup into your playgrounds. Now it's time to move beyond merely formatting the playground to making it interactive and useful. A more complex playground is created by the end of that chapter. It's shown in Listing 4-1 with one addition to the code.

At the end of Chapter 3, the playground is completed to demonstrate the use of optionals. Listing 4-1 and Figure 4-3 show the code from Chapter 3 with one addition. To recap, the playground declares an Int variable (birthYear) as an optional. This means it might be nil. In Chapter 3 you saw how the playground behaves if it is set to 21 (that is, not an optional) or if it's not set. In the addition in Listing 4-1 and Figure 4-3, the line of code to set it is inserted.

The basic playground then checks to see if birthYear is not equal to nil, and if it isn't, it is printed. Finally, myBirthYear uses optional chaining to be set either to the non-optional value or not: if the value is nil, the if statement isn't executed.

Listing 4-1. Using an Optional with Optional Binding

```
var birthYear:Int?

// birthYear = 21 DO NOT SET

birthYear = 21

if birthYear != nil {
  print (birthYear!)
}

if let myBirthYear = birthYear {
  print (myBirthYear)
}
```

Playground

• noun: a place where people can play

```
5
6 var birthYear:Int?
7
8 // birthYear = 21 DO NOT SET
9
10 birthYear = 21
11
12 if birthYear != nil {
13    print (birthYear!)
14 }
15
16 if let myBirthYear = birthYear {
17    print (myBirthYear)
18 }
```

```
21
21
```

Figure 4-3. *Test for nil and use optional binding*

All this is pretty straightforward, but it does require a bit of explanation so that you can manipulate the playground to prove how things work. Is it possible to do that with a playground? Yes. In fact, setting up the playground so you and others can experiment with it in a guided way is one of the key objectives of playgrounds.

The next section shows you how to move interactivity into the playground itself and suggest tests and experiments to users.

■ **Note** You may see this as a way to show others how to use a playground, but interactivity like this can be just as valuable to you. This particular example is simple, but building an interactive playground for yourself can be a very valuable project. First of all, it lets you experiment in ways you may not have thought of before. (In this case, for example, using the basic playground to test which types can be coerced automatically by Swift is an additional use of the code.) Beyond that, adding interactivity and text to the playground can be very useful when you come back to it in a month or two from now and want to use it.

But notice one last change you can make before moving on: changing the subtitle so that it's correct, as you see in Figure 4-4.

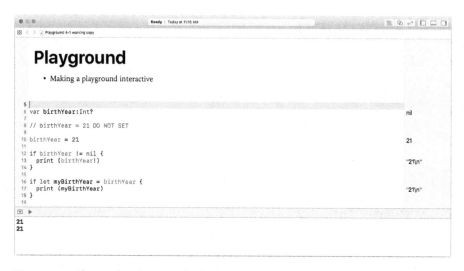

Figure 4-4. *Change the playground title*

Don't get in the habit of putting off these minor changes. Before long, they mount up, and pretty soon it's a big job to add them back in (if you can even remember the steps you've taken).

Moving a Playground from Xcode/Mac to Playgrounds/iPad

The most straightforward way to move this playground to an iOS device is to make sure it's saved to disk. Start by turning on your iOS device and checking that it's on the same WiFi network as your Mac. It doesn't have to be logged in with the same Apple ID, but it does need to be logged in.

Xcode normally keeps track of your changes and keeps them saved, but it doesn't hurt to specifically use File ➤ Save to save the playground. Locate it in the Finder and select it (a single click will do—you don't need to open it with a double-click). Once it's selected in the Finder, use the Share button in the Finder toolbar and AirDrop to move it to your iOS device, as shown in Figure 4-5. You'll be prompted to choose the user you want to share with. (If you haven't done this very often, you may have to refer to the online help for AirDrop, but once you've done it a few times, it's very natural and simple.)

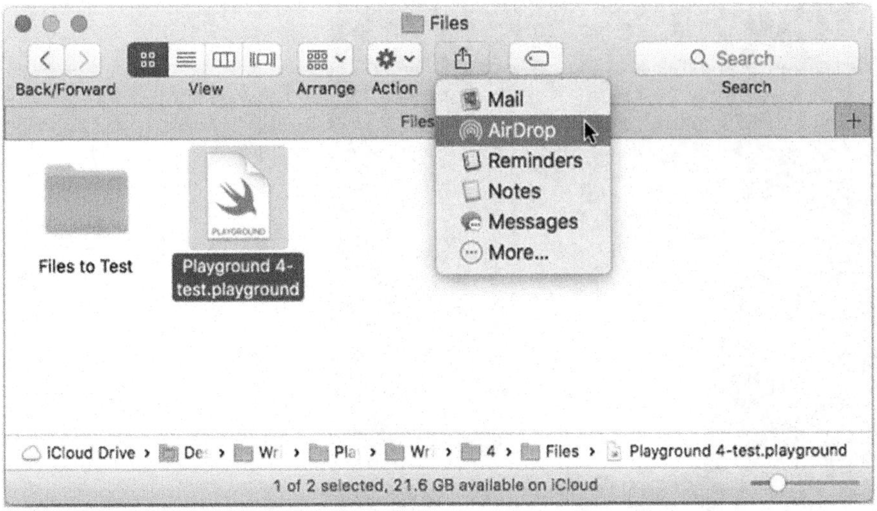

Figure 4-5. *Use AirDrop to move a file*

You'll need to choose where you want to send the file, as shown in Figure 4-6.

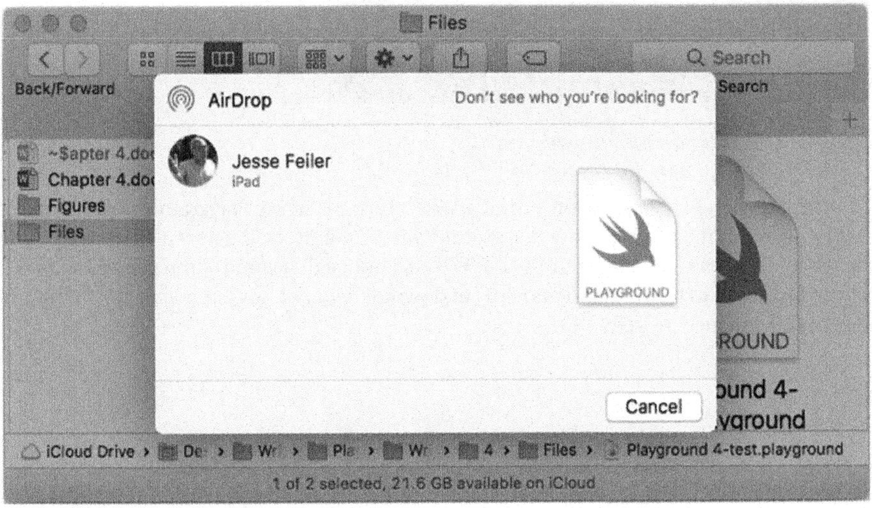

Figure 4-6. *Select the AirDrop destination*

On the iOS device, you'll be asked to receive the document, as you see in Figure 4-7.

47

Figure 4-7. *Receive an AirDrop document*

If you launch Playgrounds on your iPad (or return to the My Playgrounds view with the four boxes in the top left of the Playgrounds view), you'll see the new playground marked as New, as shown in Figure 4-8. You'll also notice that some of the playgrounds may be indicated to be in iCloud and not yet downloaded. For now, concentrate on the playground you just created.

Figure 4-8. *Playgrounds indicates playground files that are in iCloud or that are new to your device*

When you first open a foreign file, you'll be asked to confirm that it's okay, as shown in Figure 4-9.

Figure 4-9. *Confirm that you want to open an AirDrop document*

The playground opens in the Playgrounds app on iOS, as you see in Figure 4-10.

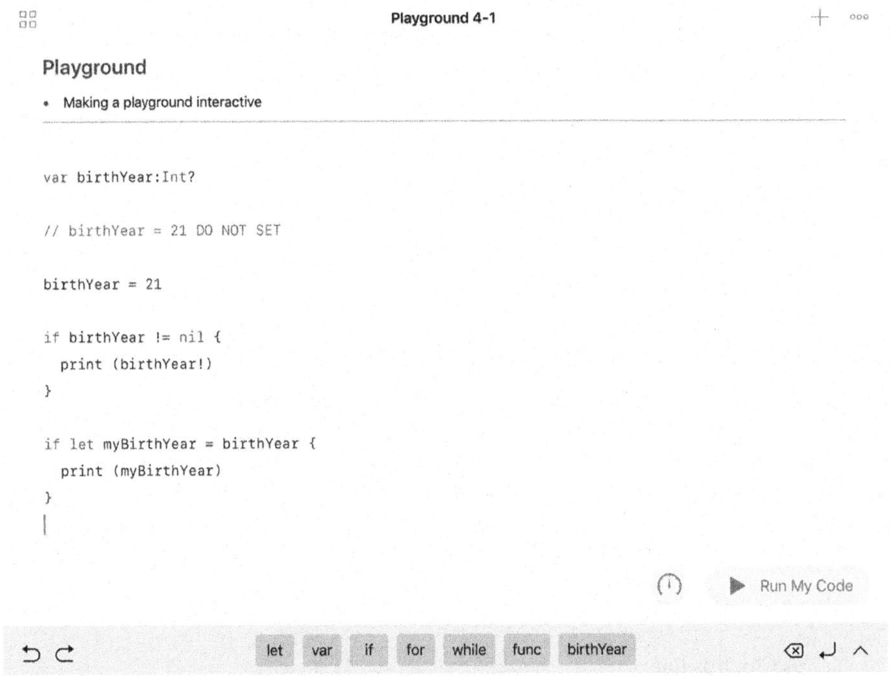

Figure 4-10. Open a playground that has been copied to your iPad with AirDrop

Compare Figure 4-10 (Playgrounds on iOS) with the same playground shown in Xcode on Mac (refer to Figure 4-4). There are some differences, particularly with the shortcuts above where the keyboard will appear. Those are discussed in Chapter 5.

Managing Interaction in a Playground

The simplest form of interaction is to move the variable assignments that you would test manually into the interactive playground. In this case, it means setting `birthYear` interactively. It would also make sense to remove the comment `DO NOT SET`.

You already have a halfway interactive playground in any playground you create: the code you type in is executed, and you can see the result. To make it more interactive, you need to be able to type in parts of code (such as the values for variables) and have what you type become part of a computation.

The simplest interaction relies on the markup functionality that you've already used, but you need to use some new commands to get data from the playground user:

- *Editable area*: An area of playground code into which the user can type code.

- *Placeholder token*: A placeholder for something the user will type in. (A placeholder token can only be placed inside an editable area.) Chapter 5 talks more about placeholder tokens.

Both are described in the sections that follow.

Creating and Using an Editable Area

An editable area is just that: an area that contains code which can be edited. You can limit the interaction within an editable area so that not everything is editable. What may be most important is that once you create an editable area in a playground, nothing else is editable in that playground. (You can have multiple editable areas and wind up making the entire playground editable in various ways.)

An editable area is delimited with special markup. It begins with a line like this:

```
//#-editable-code
```

It ends with this line:

```
//#-end-editable-code
```

Listing 4-2 shows a new playground. The code is very simple. It sets a variable to 2 and then proceeds to multiply it by 2, and later on add 4 to it and multiply it by 2. A number of print statements are interspersed.

This collection of simple lines of code forms a playground that you can use to experiment with. For example, you could change x to be 3 and multiply it by 4.5. The possibilities are endless, but you'll see a few of them in the interactive playground that follows.

Listing 4-2. A Basic Playground

```
/*:
 # Playground
 * Making a playground interactive
 */

var x = 2
x = 2 * x
print (x)

print (x)
```

```
x += 4 * 2
print (x)

print (x)
```

Using the code to delimit an editable area, you can create the playground shown in Figure 4-11.

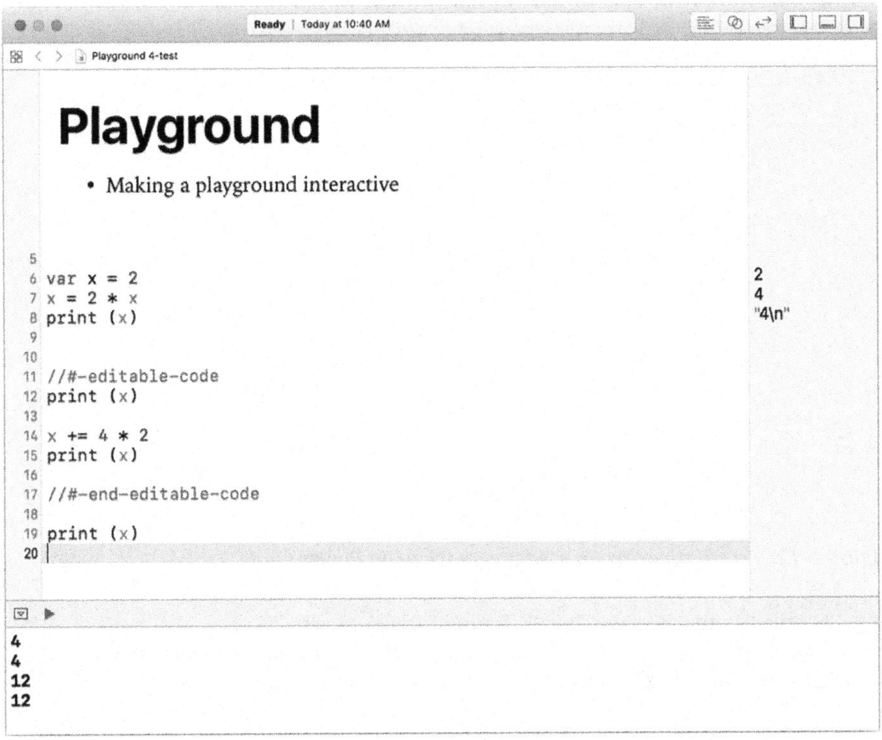

Figure 4-11. *An editable area in rendered markup in Xcode*

Move it to your iPad with AirDrop and run it in Playgrounds there, and you'll see the editable area, as shown in Figure 4-12.

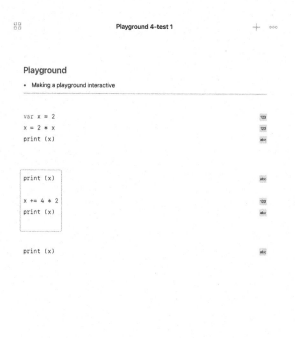

Figure 4-12. *An editable area in rendered markup on Playgrounds*

The editable area is automatically framed, as you can see.

For each of the results shown in the right-hand side, you can tap them to see the value of the numeric (123) or string (abc) viewer, as shown in Figure 4-13.

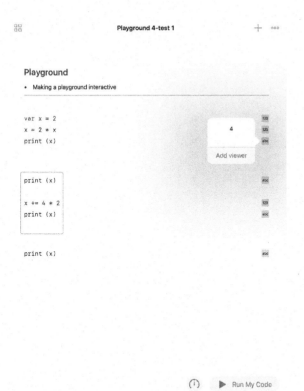

Figure 4-13. *View results in the sidebar in Playgrounds*

If you choose to add a viewer, it will show up as you see in Figure 4-14.

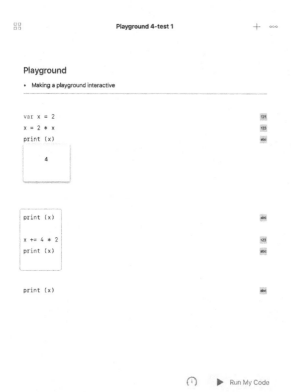

Figure 4-14. *Use a viewer in Playgrounds*

If you tap an editable area, you'll see a menu of choices, as shown in Figure 4-15. You'll also see the keyboard and be able to edit the highlighted text.

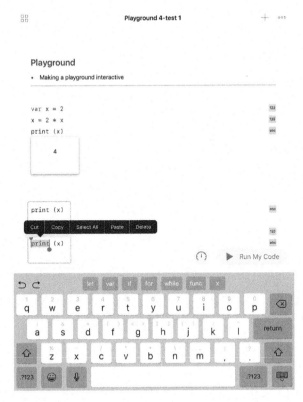

Figure 4-15. *Edit code in an editable area on Playgrounds*

When you have a viewer open, you can select its contents, as shown in Figure 4-16.

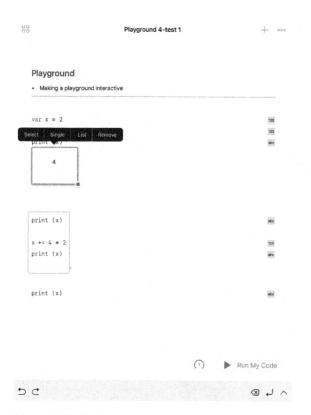

Figure 4-16. *Tap in a viewer to see options on Playgrounds*

If you select content inside a non-editable area, you have different menu options, as you can see in Figure 4-17.

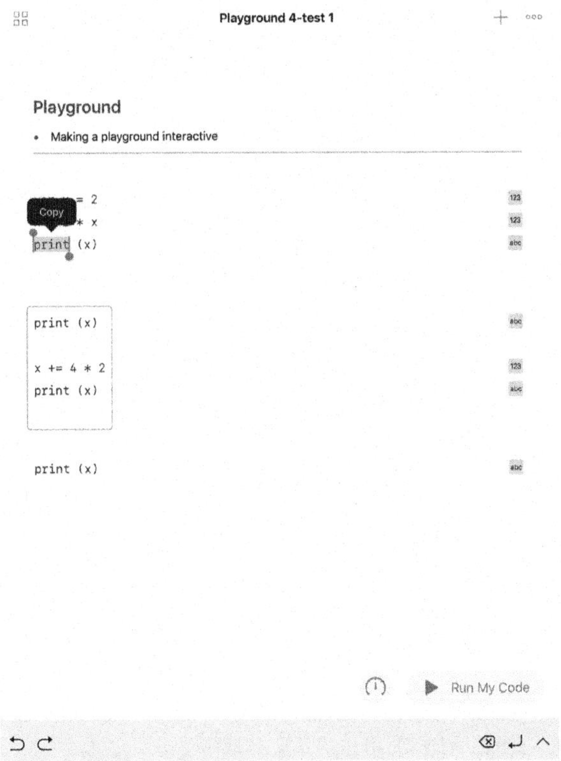

Playground 4-test 1   +   ∘∘∘

Playground

• Making a playground interactive

```
        = 2
Copy  * x
print (x)
```

```
print (x)

x += 4 * 2
print (x)
```

```
print (x)
```

⊙   ▶ Run My Code

↶ ↷   ⊗ ↵ ∧

Figure 4-17. *Menu choices in a non-editable area on Playgrounds*

But notice what you don't see: there's no keyboard. Your menu choices just let you view or even copy the data, but you can't edit it. It's not inside an editable area.

If you select something inside an editable area, you'll have other choices. For example, highlighting a number as in Figure 4-18 lets you choose to enter another number from a numeric keypad. Playgrounds constrains your choices to what is logical and syntactically correct.

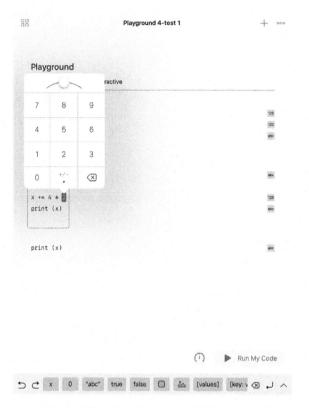

Figure 4-18. *Edit a number in an editable area on Playgrounds*

Tap in the background of an editable area, as in Figure 4-19. You see the keyboard, but you also have choices of logical syntax in the Shortcut Bar above the keyboard.

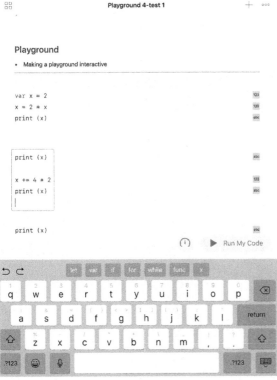

Figure 4-19. *The keyboard appears in Playgrounds when it is appropriate*

In this example, just tap `let` to begin an assignment statement. Figure 4-20 shows what that one tap does:

- `let` is inserted.

- The required syntax (`name` = `value`) is shown.

- Both `name` and `value` are highlighted so that you know to replace them with your own values and variables.

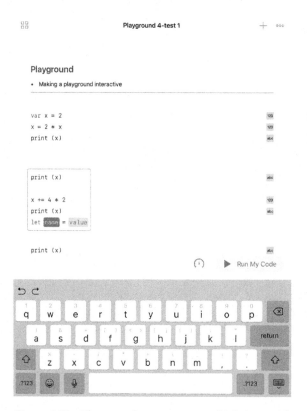

Figure 4-20. *Playgrounds can suggest multiple items to be entered*

Explore the other features of Playgrounds to start writing whatever code you want, as shown in Figure 4-21.

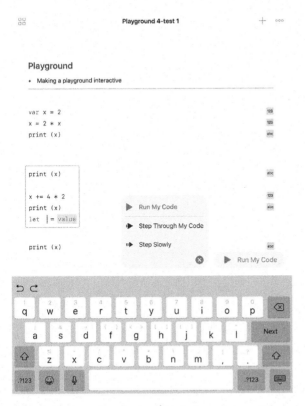

Figure 4-21. *Explore the Run My Code options on Playgrounds*

Summary

This chapter showed you how to move playgrounds back and forth between a Mac and iPad using AirDrop. You also saw how to use editable areas in markup to allow users to enter simple values such as numbers, or even free-format code of any length. You also saw the use of taps (iPad) or clicks (Mac) to bring up different menu bars depending on the context, and learned that in an editable area, the menu choices differ from those outside an editable area.

CHAPTER 5

Editing Playgrounds on iOS

Once you have a playground—written by you or others on macOS using Xcode—you can use it with the Playgrounds app on your iPad. This is a very different process from using Xcode. For one thing, now you're working on your iPad rather than a Mac, and you're writing the code that is going to run in the Playgrounds app.

Note that the code that you write with Xcode on your Mac runs in a playground inside Xcode on your Mac—but the playground running inside Xcode is different from a playground running in the Playgrounds app on iPad. You'll see that side of the process in this chapter.

___

■ **Tip** Two Apple technologies work together to make editing code easier on both iOS and macOS. The QuickType keyboard is a predictive keyboard that learns from your typing. QuickType for code builds in predictions used in writing code. The Shortcut Bar uses QuickType technology to help in providing shortcut suggestions.

___

The Playgrounds App User Interface and Experience

Chapter 4 (particularly Figure 4-15 onwards) showed how you can modify a playground running in the Playgrounds app. You saw how the keyboard can appear and how you can get help with suggestions for code, but the focus was on the basic playground structure and which areas are editable (remember, that's something you set in Xcode).

Now we'll look more closely at editing on Playgrounds. At the end of Chapter 4, the playground was being modified so that it looked like Figure 5-1. In Figure 5-2, you see the playground from the end of Chapter 4 as it appears in landscape (horizontal) mode on a 12.9-inch iPad Pro.

© Jesse Feiler 2017

J. Feiler, *Exploring Swift Playgrounds*, DOI 10.1007/978-1-4842-2647-6_5

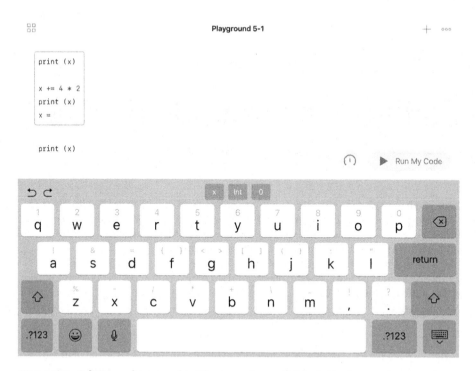

Figure 5-1. *Editing a playground in Playgrounds on a 9.7-inch iPad*

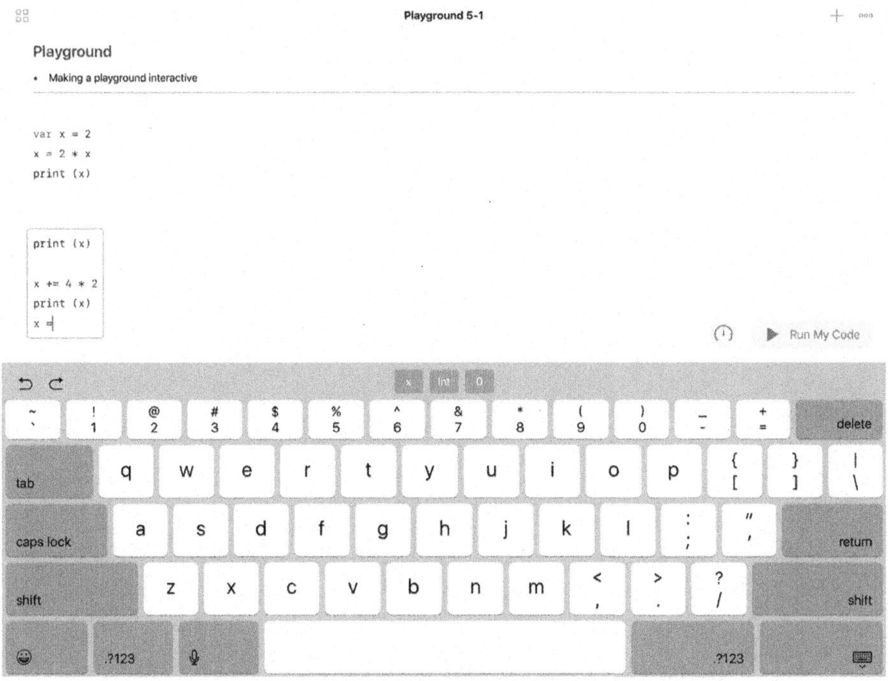

Figure 5-2. *The playground from Figure 5-1 in landscape mode on a 12.9-inch iPad*

The differences are in the keyboard, so this is a good spot to explore exactly what is in both iPad keyboards that you see in landscape mode. (In portrait—vertical—mode, there is no difference between the two iPad models.)

At the top left of both keyboards are the curved arrows for undo (left) and redo (right). In the center (the *Shortcut Bar*) are suggestions for what might be used at the current insertion point: there's more on this in the Shortcut Bar section of this chapter.

The larger iPad Pro has an additional row of keys at the top above the standard keyboard and below the Shortcut Bar. These keys (common on many standard keyboards) are the numeric keys. The Shift key lets you alternate between the numbers and symbols such as ! and @, just as on other keyboards.

On the smaller iPad Pro, that row of keys is missing. Its characters and symbols are shown in gray on the standard keyboard, and you can access them by using the ?123 key in the lower left. For keys with multiple symbols such as (, j, and) on the smaller iPad shown in Figure 5-2, swipe from one of the upper symbols on the key (for example, the (or)) to the center of the key to use the upper symbol.

On both keyboards, the small keyboard with the down-pointing arrow in the lower left hides the keyboard.

When the keyboard is hidden, a variation of the Shortcut Bar is shown at the bottom of the screen, as shown in Figure 5-3 (9.7-inch iPad Pro) and Figure 5-4 (12.9-inch iPad Pro).

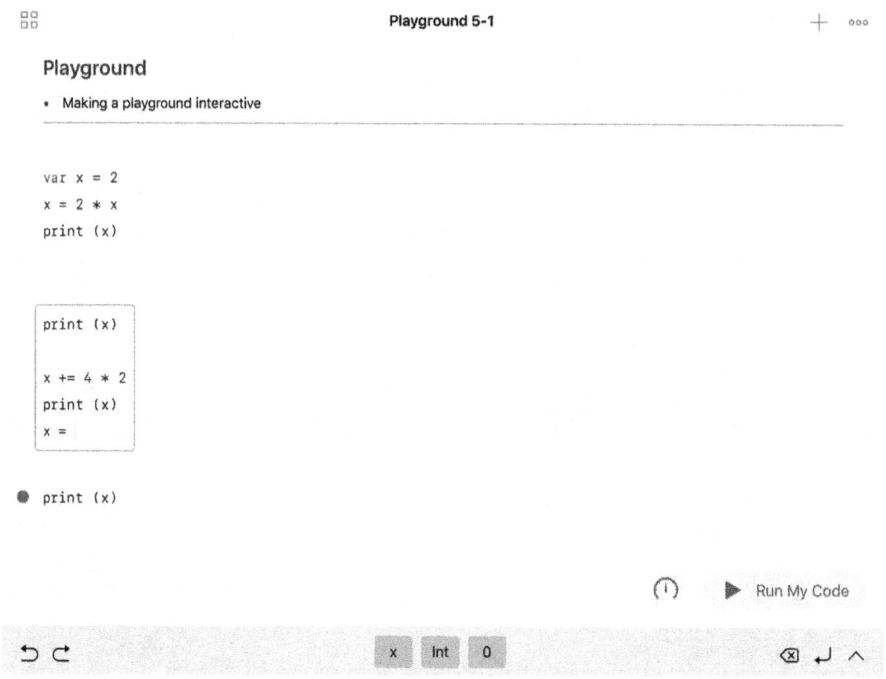
Playground 5-1
Playground
Making a playground interactive
var x = 2
x = 2 * x
print (x)
print (x)
x += 4 * 2
print (x)
x =
print (x)
Run My Code
x
Int
0

Figure 5-3. *Shortcut Bar on 9.7-inch iPad Pro*

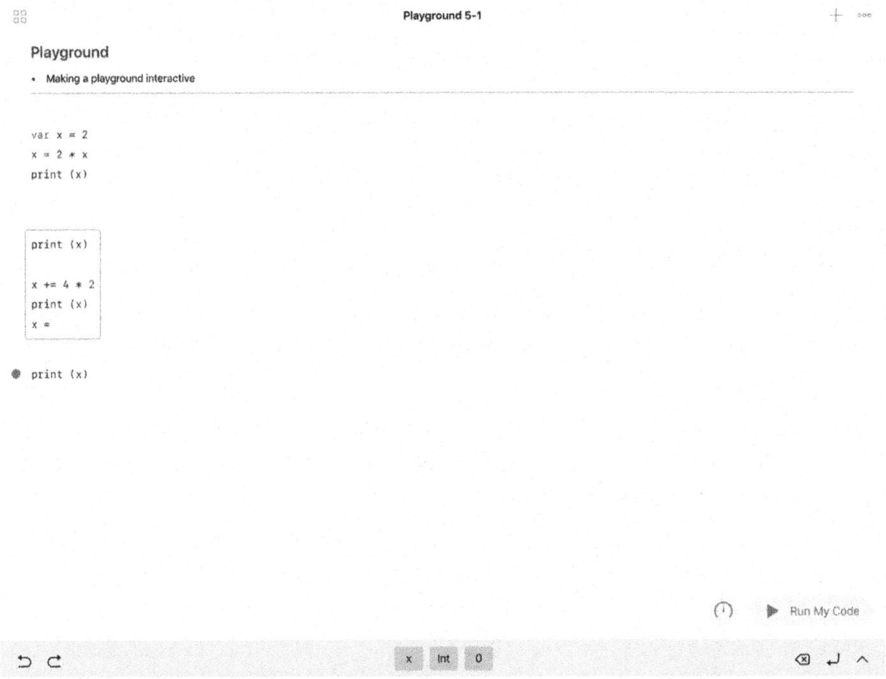

Figure 5-4. Shortcut Bar on 12.9-inch iPad Pro

Using the Shortcut Bar

The Shortcut Bar gives you suggestions of symbols that you can add to your playground code with the tap of a finger. In Figures 5-1 and 5-2, when the insertion point is placed after x = in the editable text area, your shortcut choices are x, Int, and 0. Understanding those options will let you start to see how the Shortcut Bar works.

Inserting a Simple Line of Code

In the code shown in the playground shown in the preceding figures, a variable, x, is set to 2 in the first line. Swift can infer and recognize several things from that line of code:

- x is a variable (its values can be changed if you want).

- Its initial value is 2 because that's what you set it to.

- Beyond that, Swift can infer that x is an Int because 2 is an Int. Because Swift is a strongly-typed language, it is important that each variable be typed before it is used.

With that information in the declaration and the inference from the value 2, Swift can let you proceed with your code.

Your options in the Shortcut Bar are not exhaustive, but they are often just what you need. Because x is an Int, you can set it to another Int such as 0. You can also set it to any other Int such as 17. To do so, either tap 0 and then change it to 17 or just move to the keyboard and type 17.

You can set any variable to another variable of the same type, so you certainly could set x to itself—that's the reason for the shortcut. It's a suggestion, just as 0 is a suggestion. You could set x to another variable of type Int if you already had one in your code.

Inserting More Complex Syntax

So far, you've see how to complete a simple line of code in an editable area. You can go far beyond that if you want to turn your entire playground into an editable area.

■ **Note**   This section covers such a common set of steps that you might want to bookmark this page with a note on your preferred method of transferring them (saving the playground file to your iCloud Drive or using AirDrop to transfer it).

Start with creating a basic playground in Xcode on macOS that contains an editable area and (in good practice) a title and subtitle, as you see in Figure 5-5.

```
1 /*:
2 # Open-ended Playground
3 * Write any code you want
4 */
5 //#-editable-code
6 //#-end-editable-code
7
```

Figure 5-5. *Create an editable playground in Xcode*

When you open this playground in Playgrounds on an iPad, you'll see the editable area and a prompt to tap and enter your code, as shown in Figure 5-6.

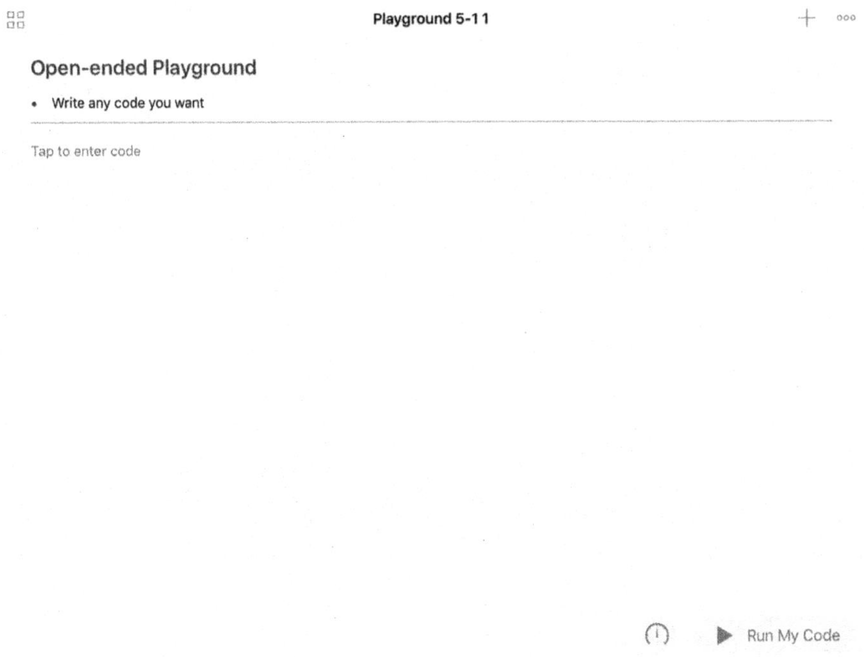

Playground 5-11   +   ooo

Open-ended Playground

• Write any code you want

Tap to enter code

(!)   ▶ Run My Code

Figure 5-6. Open the editable playground in Playgrounds on iPad

As soon as you tap to start editing, the Shortcut Bar appears, as in Figure 5-7.

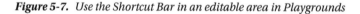

Figure 5-7. *Use the Shortcut Bar in an editable area in Playgrounds*

With an editable area, you can type anything you want, but with the Shortcut Bar, you don't need to do much typing at all. The suggestions there are usually syntactically correct, but they may not be *semantically* correct (in other words, they may not be what you want to write). There is no substitute for knowing where you're going, but a playground and the Shortcut Bar are a great substitute for checking the documentation before every keystroke. Later in this chapter you'll see two practical examples of using the Shortcut Bar to actually create some code you can use in another playground or in an Xcode app, but for now, here are some basic steps you'll use as you write that code.

Start by creating a variable and setting it. In the Shortcut Bar, tap either let or var depending on whether you want the variable to be a constant (let) or variable (var). The text created for you will be one of the following:

```
let name = value
```

or

```
var name = value
```

Both name and value are highlighted: name in gray to indicate that it is a placeholder and you must type your own name for the variable, and value in red to indicate that if you tap it you'll have further assistance in providing the value. (Figure 4-18 shows the keypad for numeric data).

As soon as you type a name of your own, the highlighting will disappear, but the red highlighting behind value will remain. In addition, the Shortcut Bar will change, as you see in Figure 5-8.

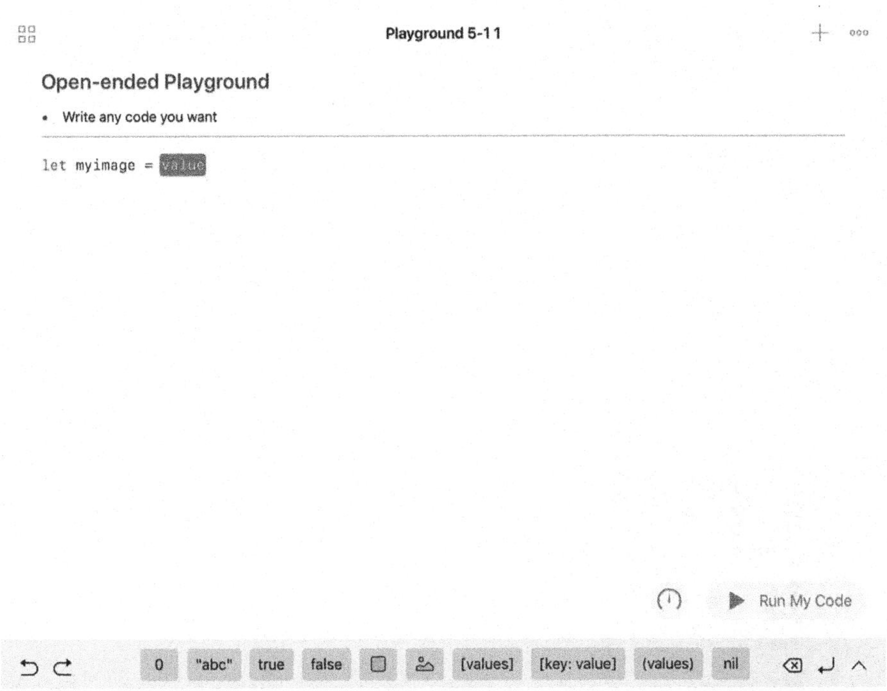

Figure 5-8. Shortcut Bar changes as you type

There are more choices now in the Shortcut Bar. From left to right they are as follows:

- 0 represents any integer (or in fact anything else you want to type there to replace the zero).

- "abc" represents a string you can change to be any string you want (or in the same way as the zero, you can retype "abc" as any value).

- true and false are the logical constants.

- The rectangle to the right of false lets you choose a color (see the "Choosing a Color" section, next).

- The image of mountain and moon/sun to the right of the color rectangle lets you select an image (see "Choosing an Image" later in this chapter).

- [values] inserts the square brackets that will surround an array or set.

- [key:value] gives you the template for creating a dictionary. The section "Putting the Pieces Together: Writing Data from an App" later in this chapter provides an example.

- (values) lets you enter a tuple.

- nil is the nil value for an optional variable (only optionals can have nil values).

Choosing a Color

If you decide to choose a color, tap the color rectangle to show the palette shown in Figure 5-9 and select the color you want.

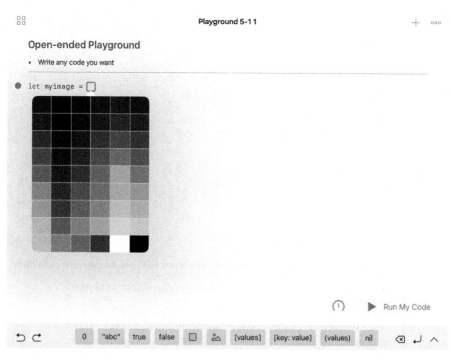

Figure 5-9. *Use the color palette with the Shortcut Bar*

Choosing an Image

If you want to set your variable to an image, tap the image button in the Shortcut Bar and you'll be able to choose the image you want, as shown in Figure 5-10.

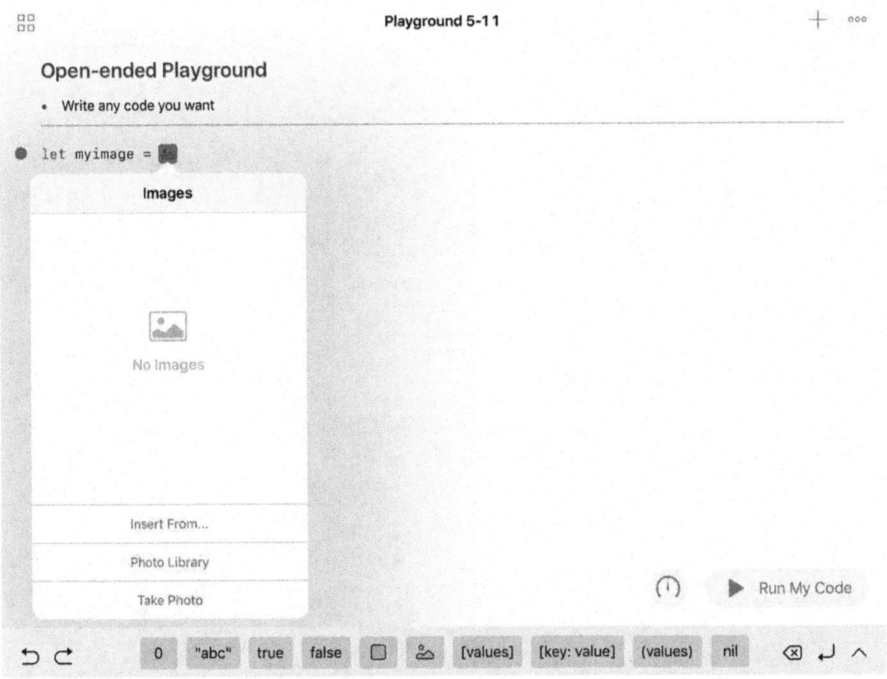

Figure 5-10. *Use an image with the Shortcut Bar*

Your choices are the standard macOS and iOS image resources: a file, your Photo Library, or your iPad's camera. Figure 5-11 shows the permissions alert you see if you choose Take Photo.

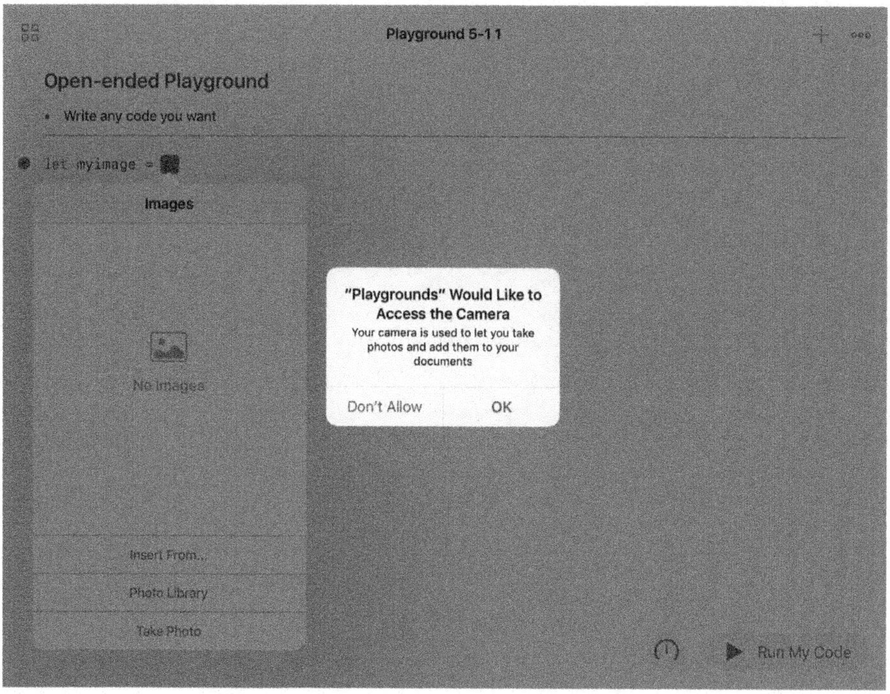

Figure 5-11. *You need permission to access the iPad's camera*

If you decide to pick a photo from your Photo Library, the standard interface you see in Figure 5-12 lets you choose what you want.

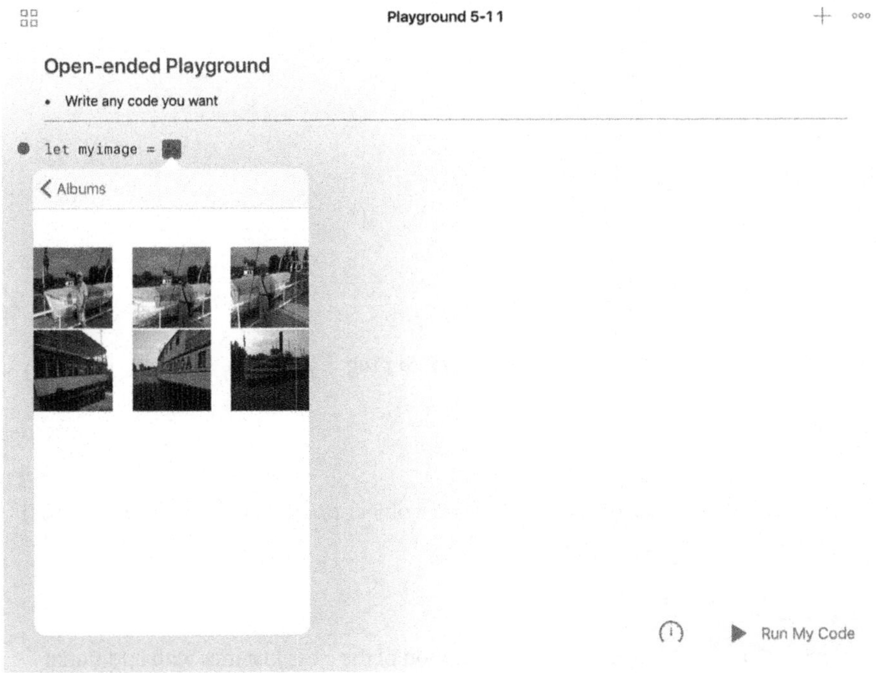

Figure 5-12. *You can choose an image from your Photo Library*

Putting the Pieces Together: Writing a Class in a Playground with the Shortcut Bar

This section discusses writing a class in a playground by typing it. In fact, that's the same way you would type it with Xcode for a traditional project. Then you'll see how to use the Shortcut Bar to do the same thing and not only save keystrokes but also let the playground coach you and remind you what your coding options are.

Typing the Code

In Chapter 3, you saw the bare bones of a Swift class (ClassName) in the "Classes, Enumerations, and Structures" section. The code for the class is repeated here (with a change in the title) in Listing 5-1.

Listing 5-1. ClassName Bare-Bones Swift Class

```
/*:
 # Playing with Classes
 * exploring classes and instances
 */

import UIKit

class ClassName {
  var myVariable: String?
  let myConstant: String? = "Something"

  func myFunction (parameter: Double) -> String {
    return "my result"
  }
}
```

As with all Swift classes (and classes in most object-oriented programing languages), you *instantiate* the class with code such as this:

```
let myInstance = ClassName()
```

Having done that, you can then use a method of the class instance with additional code, like this:

```
let theResult = myInstance.myFunction (parameter: 17.2)
```

And you will get the response back as "my result" because at this point the class's method returns a constant string.

You can add a class function to the class: a *class function* is a function of the class itself rather than an instance of the class. A class function is prefixed by the keyword class:

```
class func myClassFunction
```

You can then call that function on the class without having an instance.

Figure 5-13 shows the code shown previously with a class function added. You can see the class description with the class function and the instance function within it. Below the class, you see the creation of a class instance (myInstance), the result of calling a function on the instance (myInstance.myFunction), and the result of calling a class method on the class (ClassName.myClassFunction).

```
 1  /*:
 2  # Playing with Classes
 3  * exploring classes and instances
 4  */
 5
 6  import UIKit
 7
 8  class ClassName {
 9    var myVariable: String?
10    let myConstant: String? = "Something"
11
12    class func myClassFunction (parameter: Int) -> String {
13      return "myClassFunction returns " + String (parameter)     "myClassFunction returns -37"
14    }
15
16    func myFunction (parameter: Double) -> String {
17      return "myFunction returns " + String (parameter)          "myFunction returns 17.2"
18    }
19  }
20
21  let myInstance = ClassName()                                      ClassName
22  let theResult = myInstance.myFunction(parameter: 17.2)           "myFunction returns 17.2"
23  let theClassResult = ClassName.myClassFunction (parameter: Int(-37.1))  "myClassFunction returns -37"
24
```

Figure 5-13. *Use a class method*

Using the Shortcut Bar to Write the Code

Particularly if you're a fast typist and know Swift very well, the Shortcut Bar may seem unnecessary, and it may even seem as if it slows you down. In practice, many developers (including the author) use a combination of typing, knowledge of Swift, and the Shortcut Bar. This section covers a few steps to show you how to integrate the Shortcut Bar with writing code, such as that shown in Figure 5-13.

Creating an Empty Playground

Begin with an empty playground, created in Playgrounds on your iPad. To begin with, the comments, title, and subtitle at the top of the playground in Figure 5-13 aren't necessary for this example, so they're not included. Also UIKit isn't used here, so although it's part of a playground created in Xcode, it's not part of a playground created on your iPad. Create a new playground with the + from the My Playgrounds library, as you see in Figure 5-14. (If you need to get back to the library, the four boxes in the top left will take you there.)

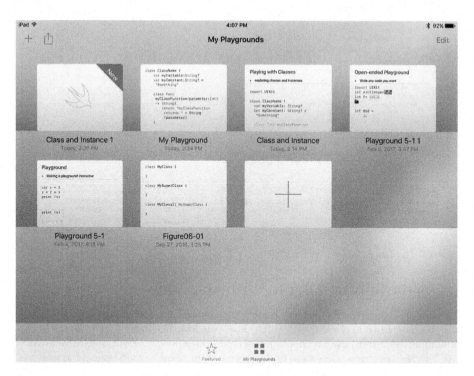

Figure 5-14. *Create a new playground on iPad with Playgrounds*

If you're looking at another view, such as a playground itself rather than the library, the four-square button in the top left of the screen will take you to the library, as shown in Figure 5-15.

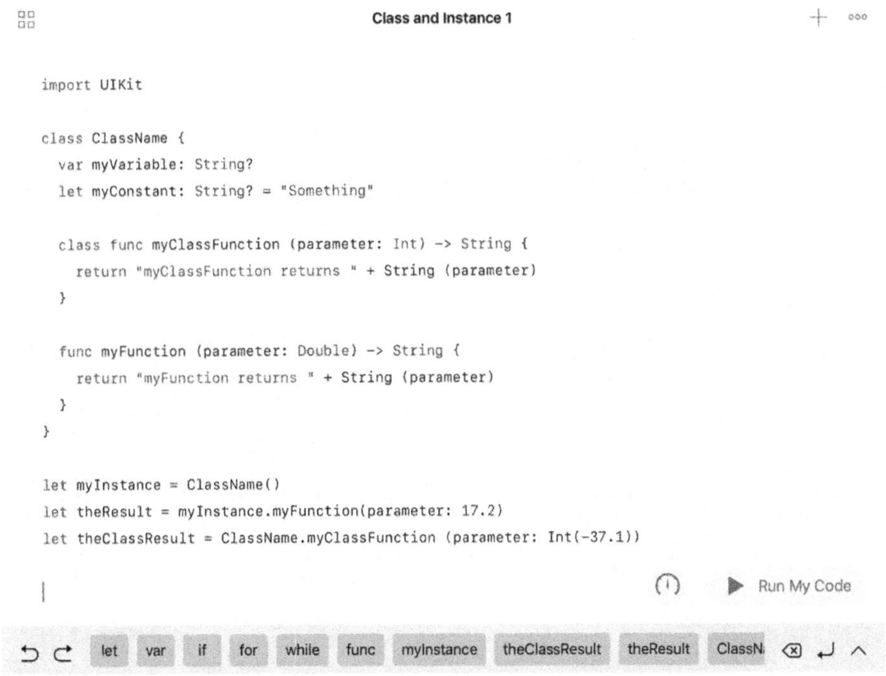

Class and Instance 1

```
import UIKit

class ClassName {
  var myVariable: String?
  let myConstant: String? = "Something"

  class func myClassFunction (parameter: Int) -> String {
    return "myClassFunction returns " + String (parameter)
  }

  func myFunction (parameter: Double) -> String {
    return "myFunction returns " + String (parameter)
  }
}

let myInstance = ClassName()
let theResult = myInstance.myFunction(parameter: 17.2)
let theClassResult = ClassName.myClassFunction (parameter: Int(-37.1))
```

Run My Code

let   var   if   for   while   func   myInstance   theClassResult   theResult   ClassN

Figure 5-15. *The completed playground as it will be at the end of this chapter*

Show the Keyboard and Handle the Red Dot

From a new blank playground, begin by showing the keyboard with the up-arrow at the right of the Shortcut Bar, as you see in Figure 5-15. If the keyboard is shown, the up- or down-arrow is at the right of the bottom row of keys. Type a single character on the empty playground view: type *c* (for *class*), as shown in Figure 5-16.

Figure 5-16. *Start typing code*

You can type directly onto the empty playground view, but for a blank playground your choices for the Shortcut Bar may not be the ones you want. It's usually best to show the keyboard and type the first character of the first line you want to write.

■ **Note**   Yes, that's circular—how do you know what you want to type? A double-tap on an empty playground will populate the Shortcut Bar with the most common beginnings, but a class is not one of them. (The common beginnings that will be shown in the Shortcut Bar are let, var, if, for, while, and func.)

As you see in Figure 5-16, if you type a *c*, you'll soon see a red dot at the left (in the *gutter*). That indicates an error, so tap it to see what it is. The message is that it's an unresolved identifier, but the Shortcut Bar has now expanded to show you new options that start with *c*, and class is one of them.

In practice, once you get used to the keyboard, here's how you start from a blank playground to create a class:

1.   Type *c*.

2.   Tap class in the Shortcut Bar.

Before long, you won't even look at the Shortcut Bar to watch its changes. You'll just type something (often more than one character) and then look directly at the Shortcut Bar to see what your choices are. It really is much faster to do than describe. Note that forcing yourself to go step-by-step to watch the Shortcut Bar change will probably take you longer than just taking a chance. Remember, the undo button in the top left of the keyboard is always there for you.

Complete the Class Definition

After you tap class in the Shortcut Bar, you'll get the shell of the class, as you see in Figure 5-17. You'll see this type of structure frequently in a playground: functions start out looking much like classes. The name of the object (class or function) is highlighted in red; you need to provide the name of it. The placeholder for code has a gray background; you replace the placeholder with one or more lines of code.

Figure 5-17. *The snippet for a class is generated automatically*

To enter the name of the object, you won't be able to rely on QuickType because the name can be anything, and there's nothing for QuickType to use to complete your typing. So you'll need to tap the red-highlighted name and type in a new name such as ClassName, as shown in Figure 5-18.

83

Figure 5-18. Enter your own class name

Moving down to the code placeholder, you may want to enter the var declaration of myVariable (as shown in Figure 5-15). Just type the *v* of var as you see in Figure 5-19. You'll see the red error dot because your code is not complete, but the Shortcut Bar quickly changes to give you two options beginning with *v*—a string starting with *v* and the keyword var, which is what you want, so just tap that.

Figure 5-19. *QuickType knows the symbols you have created*

As you continue entering the code for your class and its class function, you'll switch back and forth between typing and using the Shortcut Bar suggestions. For example, if you continue to add a type annotation for myVariable, you'll need to type the colon, but having done so, you'll see in the Shortcut Bar the various types you can use, as shown in Figure 5-20.

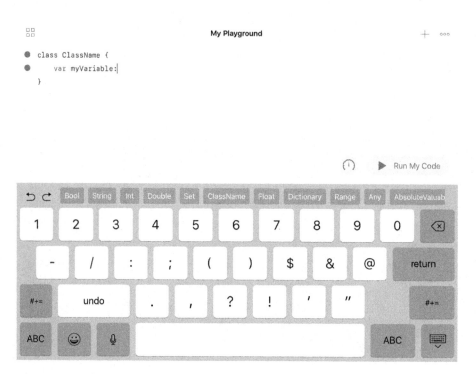

Figure 5-20. *The Shortcut Bar shows you possible types for a variable declaration*

When you get down to entering the class function, as soon as you type the *c*,
QuickType will suggest a class declaration, as shown in Figure 5-21.

Figure 5-21. *QuickType can work even with a single character that you type*

But as soon as you type just the *f* for func, the Shortcut Bar gives you the choices shown in Figure 5-22, and you're on your way.

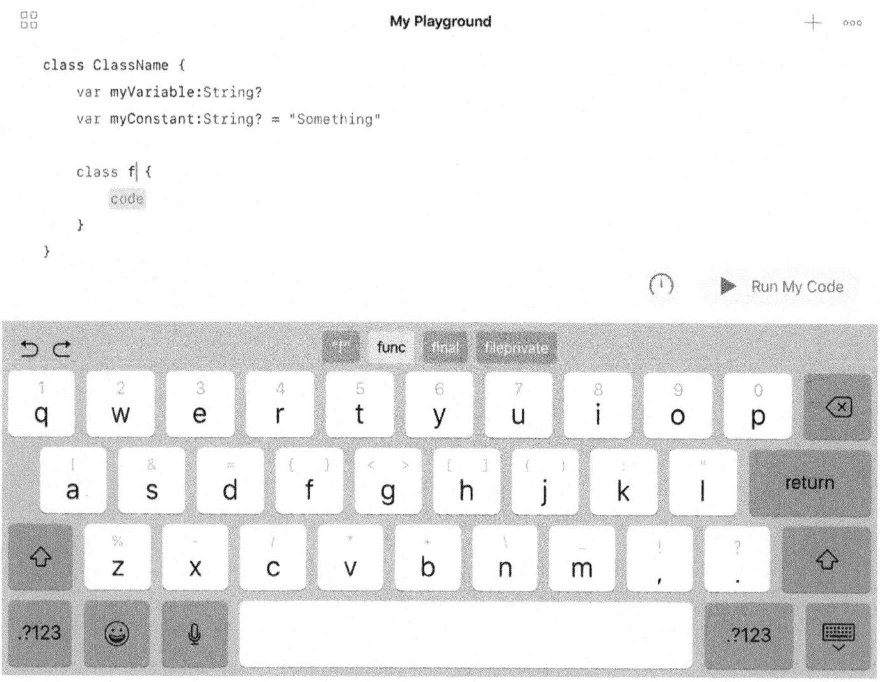
My Playground
class ClassName {
var myVariable:String?
var myConstant:String? = "Something"
class f {
code
}
}
Run My Code
"f"
func
final
fileprivate
return
.?123
.?123

Figure 5-22. *The Shortcut Bar adjusts for each additional character you type*

Continue on in this way, bouncing between the keyboard and the Shortcut Bar. Once you start using the Shortcut Bar, you'll find it's a big time saver, and the code it writes with you will be syntactically correct, although you have to make certain that the syntax is what you're trying to create.

When you have reconstructed the code for this example, you can run it in your playground and show the results, as you can see in Figure 5-23.

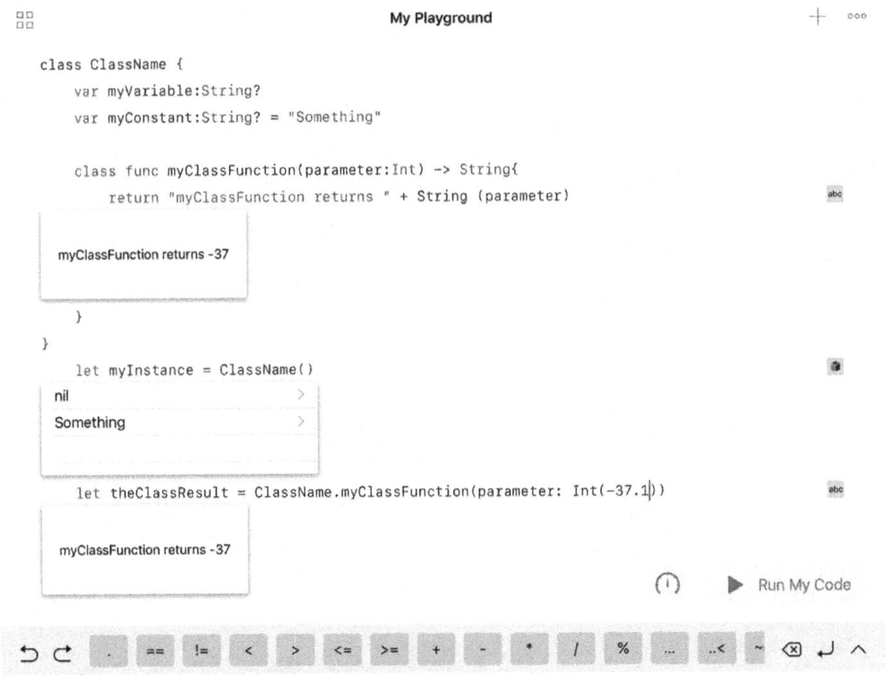

Figure 5-23. *Try out your new playground on iPad*

Summary

This chapter shows you the interplay between your typing (often not much of it) and the Shortcut Bar's suggestions. The suggestions are both context sensitive in that the Swift syntax is parsed as you go along and the suggestions are usually valid syntax. The suggestions also reflect your own data (the names of your symbols, for example).

Together these technologies can make your code more robust as well as speed up the typing and debugging steps.

CHAPTER 6

Entering Data and Viewing Results in Swift Playgrounds

You can use playgrounds to test your own code and try out experiments, but that's just the beginning. Instead of experimenting by changing code and rerunning your playground, you can set it up so that you (or others) can enter data and then have the playground code act on the data.

To do that, you need to be able to control what is shown in the playground's timeline and current view as it executes, and that's what this chapter shows you how to do. You'll see how to view a playground's timeline and current view in Xcode as well as Playgrounds (the app on iPad). Using the current view in this way opens up many opportunities for your own experimentation as well as possibilities for teaching, documenting code and processes in your organization, and many other opportunities.

You'll also see that you can draw in the current view as well as how to use view and other graphical components of UIKit to build very powerful interfaces that you can then move into another app or even into a playground.

■ **Note** In this book, the playgrounds you're seeing are all a single playground page in length. There's plenty to do with playground pages like this (particularly because in the digital world, the pages can be as long as you want them to be). If you want to move on, you can create playground books. On http://developer.apple.com search for "Playground Book Package" and you'll see how to build multi-page playgrounds along the lines of Apple's Learn to Code and other playgrounds. Even when you move on to playground books, you'll still be working on a single page at a time (along with a few other components you can put into a playground book). In Chapter 9, you'll see how to build multi-page playgrounds that are midway in complexity between playground books and one-page playgrounds.

© Jesse Feiler 2017
J. Feiler, *Exploring Swift Playgrounds*, DOI 10.1007/978-1-4842-2647-6_6

Using the Timeline

The playground timeline lets you look at the state of your playground over time. In previous chapters, you've seen how to use the `print` statement to show values of variables and, if you want, to print out strings that you create to annotate what's going on.

■ **Note** Swift 3 and Xcode 8 changed a number of important features in playgrounds. They are shown in the figures in this chapter. Older examples and documentation may no longer work, but the API we now have for timelines and Swift should be stable going forward.

If you have a repetition statement such as a loop, you'll see the number of repetitions in the sidebar, but you won't see the values as shown in Figure 6-1 running a playground on macOS in Xcode.

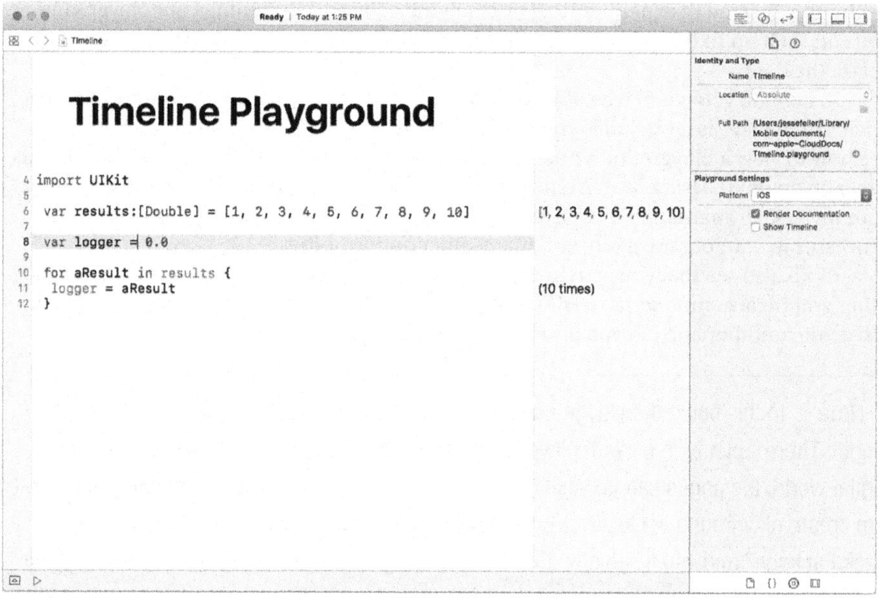

Figure 6-1. *Watch the sidebar to see repetitions*

You might notice at the right of Figure 6-1 that the right-hand utilities pane of the Xcode workspace window is exposed, and the File pane is selected so you can see the file's location. There are two playground-specific settings you can choose:

- The Render Documentation check box has the same effect as the Editor ➤ Show Raw/Rendered Markup command.

- The Show Timeline check box will show a timeline at the bottom of the main playground window. It is turned off in Figure 6-1.

You can view the results within the for loop (or any other repetition structure) by clicking the Quick Look button at the right of the sidebar, as shown in Figure 6-2.

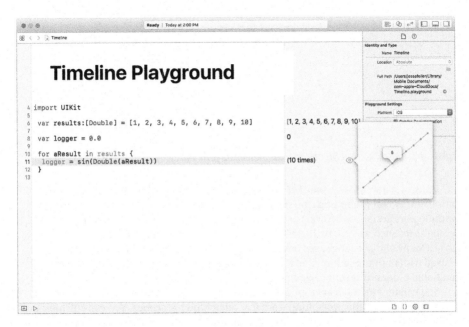

Figure 6-2. *Use Quick Look to see the reptitions in the timeline*

The Quick Look result is interactive—you can click a dot to see its value.

Alternatively, you can add a result viewer to the playground with the button to the right of Quick Look, as shown in Figure 6-3.

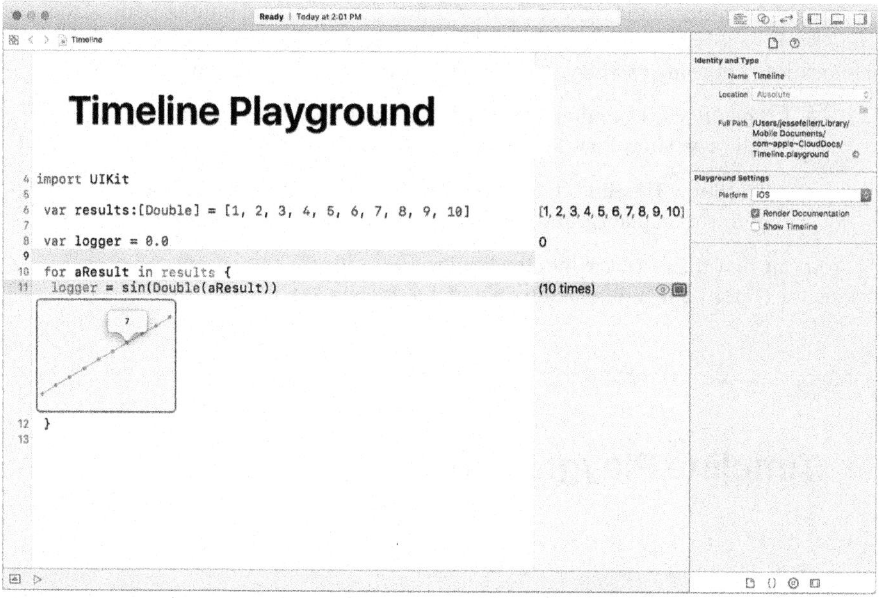

Figure 6-3. *Add the timeline to a result viewer in your playground*

Control statements such as for, while, and do loops are the mainstays of *procedural* (or *imperative*) programming (the style of *do this, do that*). Functional programming has become more and more central to software development since its widespread adoption by languages such as Perl, PHP, Haskell, C#, Java, and now Swift, from the 1980s through today. (Many of those languages began as procedural languages and today can now be used with both procedural and functional programming styles.) There is more on functional programming in Chapter 9.

You can rewrite the playground as functional code, as shown in Figure 6-4. The map function handles all the procedural work for you behind the scenes. You can still look at each value, but the interface shown in Figure 6-4 running on an iPad is different.

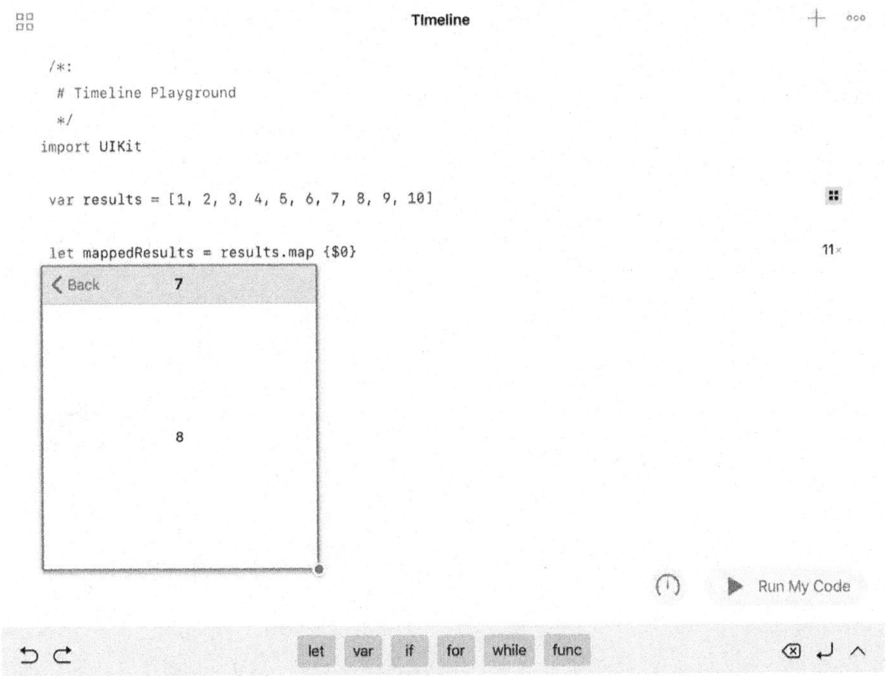

```
/*:
 # Timeline Playground
 */
import UIKit

var results = [1, 2, 3, 4, 5, 6, 7, 8, 9, 10]

let mappedResults = results.map {$0}
```

Timeline

11×

< Back   7

8

Run My Code

let   var   if   for   while   func

Figure 6-4. Use the map *function for a functional approach to repetition*

■ **Tip**   As you will see in Chapter 9, the key implementations of functional programming are the map, filter, and reduce functions. map and filter loop through each element in a collection to either use them in a calculation (map) or test them for inclusion in a new collection (filter). reduce loops through them to derive a single value using the algorithm you specify.

Timelines are a powerful and useful way of monitoring the execution of your playground.

Creating a Basic Playground with a View

The first step in providing interactivity in your playground is to show a current view. The second step will be to add interactivity to that view.

As always, begin with a playground. The playground used in this chapter is shown both in Xcode and Playgrounds in this section, but the code is basically irrelevant to which platform you're using. (There definitely *are* some differences that will be pointed out, but mostly the code is the code.)

The playground you see in Figure 6-5, which I'll call Interactive Playground, is the basis for this chapter, shown here on Xcode.

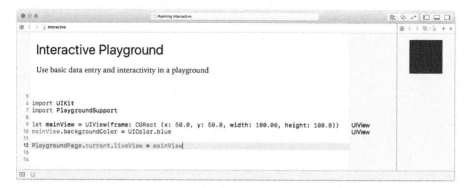

***Figure 6-5.** Interactive Playground with a view*

Enter the code shown in Listing 6-1 and show the Assistant.

***Listing 6-1.** Show View in Your Playground's Current Live View*

```
/*:
 ## Interactive Playground
 Use basic data entry and interactivity in a playground
 */

import UIKit
import PlaygroundSupport

let mainView = UIView(frame: CGRect
  (x: 50.0, y: 50.0, width: 100.00, height: 100.0))
mainView.backgroundColor = UIColor.blue

PlaygroundPage.current.liveView = mainView
```

After the initial title and subtitle you import UIKit, which is needed any time you need the basic interface elements in a playground. You also need to import PlaygroundSupport, the module that supports interactive playgrounds.

Inside every interactive playground that you build, you'll need to have a view into which you can draw. In this example, it is created with this line of code:

```
let mainView = UIView(let mainView = UIView(frame: CGRect
  (x: 50.0, y: 50.0, width: 100.00, height: 100.0))
```

For future use, this view is assigned a background color of blue:

```
mainView.backgroundColor = UIColor.blue
```

Remember as you're typing that the Shortcut Bar will have your color choices as soon as you type the *UIC* of UIColor.

Finally, you need to assign the view to the playground page you're working with. Here is the line of code for that (you use this line of code in most simple cases without modification):

```
PlaygroundPage.current.liveView = mainView
```

Looking at Your View in the Timeline

You have created a view and colored it blue, but it doesn't exist anywhere yet. The key to using it in your playground is to assign it to the current view of the playground. That's where the PlaygroundSupport module comes into play: it has a reference to the current playground page (PlaygroundPage.current). PlaygroundPage is the major class in PlaygroundSupport, and it represents exactly what its name suggests. You may actually have several PlaygroundPage instances at one time, but only one of them is current, and that's what this code snippet refers to. A PlaygroundPage can include variable data that the user enters or that is generated as the playground runs, so it is a dynamic object.

Any PlaygroundPage can have a liveView. A liveView is any object that conforms to the PlaygroundLiveViewable protocol. Those objects include UIView, UIViewController, and all their descendants—basically the user interface elements of Cocoa and Cocoa Touch. There are lots of opportunities for you here.

If you move this playground to Playgrounds on an iPad, you can run it in landscape mode, as shown in Figure 6-6. On the iPad, you'll see the color blue.

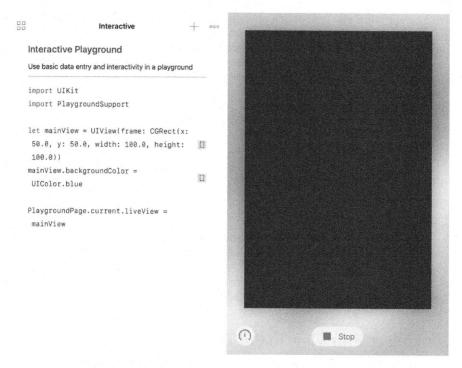

Figure 6-6. *A simple view in a playground*

▤ **Note**   Among the parts of playgrounds that have changed since the launch in 2016 are the timeline and, with it, interactions with views beyond the simple text tools you've seen in the early chapters of this book. For that reason make sure that, as you explore blogs and websites for examples of Swift playgrounds, you're using the latest versions of Swift and Playgrounds (for Mac users, that means the latest version of Xcode). In a playground, if you see `import XCPlayground`, you're looking at the older version. You should see `import PlaygroundSupport` instead. (In many playgrounds you don't need either one.)

Add a Second View to the Live View

You can enhance your playground by adding a second view. You create another view and give it a frame with dimensions in this line of code:

```
let innerView = UIView (frame: CGRect
  (x: 50.0, y: 50.0, width: 100.00, height: 100.0))
```

So you can see it easily against the blue of mainView, set its background color to green (or any color other than the background color of the main view).

```
innerView.backgroundColor = UIColor.green
```

Finally, add this to mainView, which has already been set to the page's live view:

```
mainView.addSubview(innerView)
```

■ **Tip** You may notice that the location of both views is the same, but remember that the frame's location (*x* and *y*) is relative to its superview. Furthermore, the view that's placed in the live view behaves a bit differently from views that are placed in other views and is resized as you rotate your iPad.

On Playgrounds on your iPad, when you tap Run My Code, you'll see both views in landscape mode, as shown in Figure 6-7, and in portrait mode, as in Figure 6-8. Note that the inner view maintains the dimensions you set for it; the main view is resized as you rotate your iPad.

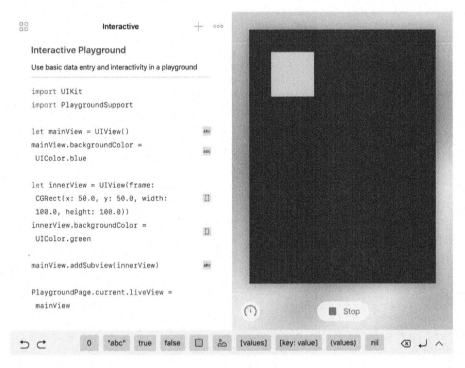

Figure 6-7. Two views in a playground (landscape mode)

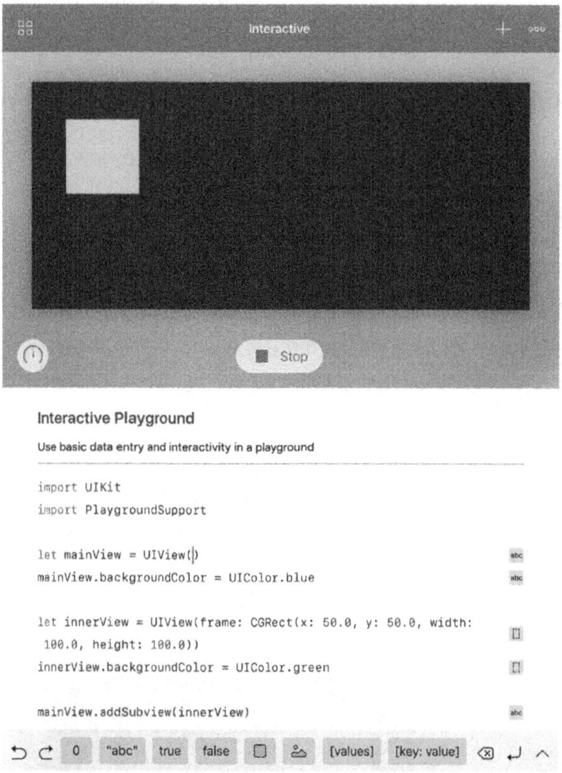

Figure 6-8. *Two views in a playground (portrait mode)*

As you might expect, on an iPad you can adjust the two views in the split view, as you see in Figure 6-9.

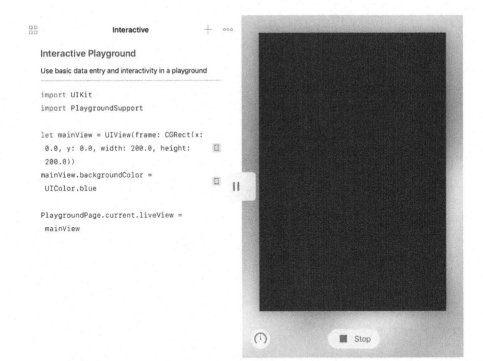

Figure 6-9. *Adjust the split view*

Working with Interactive Data Entry

Putting colored views onto the Playgrounds timeline on macOS or onto the Playgrounds app on iOS is a start, but it's really not interactive. Interactive would allow for user input and for changes in the display that are not code-based. That's what this section shows you how to do.

The preceding example shows how to create a new view and, within it, another view. The first view (containing the innerview) is then set to the playground's liveView. As noted, liveView can be set to any object that conforms to the PlaygroundLiveViewable protocol, which means that UIView and UIViewController can be used for liveView.

A view (that is, an instance of UIView) can contain other views, as is the case in this example. The view in the Interactive example is essential at the top level of the view hierarchy. (In reality, it becomes part of the view of the playground that is at the top level, but that's a digression into the mechanics of playgrounds that need not bother you at the moment.)

A view controller is designed to contain other views and, more importantly, to manage interactions between those views. A view controller itself can contain properties that are shared among its views, and that's what's going to happen here. There will be a text field into which you can enter text. What you enter will then be shown in a label field (labels in Cocoa Touch are not editable by the user, although you can modify them in code as you will do here). The view controller will contain a property for the label as well as for the text field. When editing of the text field is complete, its value (the text entered) will be placed in the label.

101

Creating a New Playground

Start by creating a new playground: DataEntry is a good name for it. You can do this either on macOS with Xcode or on iOS with Playgrounds. The process on macOS has been shown in previous chapters. To create a new playground in Playgrounds, use the + in the top left of the window to create a new playground. It will have a default name (like MyPlayground 3). Tap Edit in the top right and then select that new playground. You'll be able to enter a new name for it, and you can proceed.

Creating a View Controller for the Live View

The first step for creating a view controller in a new playground is shown in Listing 6-2.

Listing 6-2. Creating a New View Controller

```
/*:
  # Interactive Playground
  * DataEntry
  */

import UIKit
import PlaygroundSupport

class JFTextFieldController : UIViewController, UITextFieldDelegate {
  var textField: UITextField!
  var label: UILabel!
}

PlaygroundPage.current.liveView = JFTextFieldController()
```

You can place whatever title and subtitle you want at the top. Unlike the case where you use a UIView in the live view of a playground just by instantiating a UIView, you typically create a subclass of UIViewController when you want to use a view controller in a playground. The reason is that because the view controller will need to coordinate data and more than one view in many cases, you probably won't find a view controller class that exactly fits your needs for the playground.

▪ **Note**   This is not to say that you always need to override a UIViewController. There are many cases when you can use the base class or one of its subclasses in your apps or playgrounds. However, it seems that playgrounds often require a subclass of UIViewController. This is only an observation and not a requirement in any way.

In this case, the subclass of UIViewController is called JFViewController. It is a subclass of UIViewController as will be any view controller class that you create. In order to manage the text field, the class will need to conform to UITextFieldDelegate protocol. (See "Managing Text Fields" later in this chapter.)

The view controller will need two properties, one for the text field and one for the label. Their declarations are at the top of the class definition.

■ **Note** As is the case with most user interface elements, the properties of the elements are *implicitly unwrapped optionals* using the ! postfix operator on the property type. An implicitly unwrapped optional can be set to nil or its type. In the case of interface elements, they are typically nil until they are set in the instantiated interface.

An instance of JFTestFieldController is created and set to the live view of the current page, and with that the basic playground is set up, but nothing is visible and nothing is operational yet.

Creating the View Controller Views

When you directly instantiate views in a playground as shown in the Interactive Playground in the first part of this chapter, the view creation happens as your code is executed. The view controller here will do the creation of its view and any subviews that view has. (This is not always the case; subviews are sometimes created by other objects and then placed in the view controller, but the process outlined here is perhaps more common.)

VIEW SETUP SUMMARY

The following are the methods that a view controller uses to set up itself and its views. loadView() is called when the view controller itself is loaded. You may override loadView() to create subviews and do anything else to initialize the view controller right at the start. Companion methods viewWillLoad() and viewDidLoad() are called before and after loadView().

Two other sets of methods are called later on: viewWillAppear() and its companion viewDidAppear() are called first, and later viewWillDisappear() and viewDidDisappear() are called. Appearing and disappearing happen after a view has been loaded. Override loadView() or its companions for one-time setup, and use the appearance methods to modify the data shown by a loaded view or, in the case of disappearance, to save it to a persistent store.

Creating the subviews is done in the loadView() method in the DataEntry playground shown in Listing 6-3. (loadView is a stub at this point.)

Listing 6-3. Add loadView()

```
class JFTextFieldController : UIViewController, UITextFieldDelegate {
    var textField: UITextField!
    var label: UILabel!
```

```
override func loadView() {
 }

}
```

```
PlaygroundPage.current.liveView = JFTextFieldController()
```

The code will be basically the same as you have seen in the Interactive Playground:

1. Create an instance of a view.

2. Set its frame.

3. Set its color(s) if necessary as well as any other properties you need.

These are the basic steps in creating any view programmatically (as opposed to using a storyboard). For views that are to be shown in a playground, you add them as subviews to the view that becomes part of the playground.

Creating the Main View Subview

Listing 6-4 shows the code to create the main view, called view for the sake of simplicity. You can name it anything you want.

Listing 6-4. Creating the Main View

```
let view = UIView(frame: CGRect(x: 50, y: 50, width: 100, height: 100))
view.backgroundColor = UIColor.cyan
```

That listing is identical to the code you've seen previously in this chapter, but as you type it you may want to try something new using QuickType. As you start typing the *CGRect*, you're presented with possible completions, as you can see in Figure 6-10.

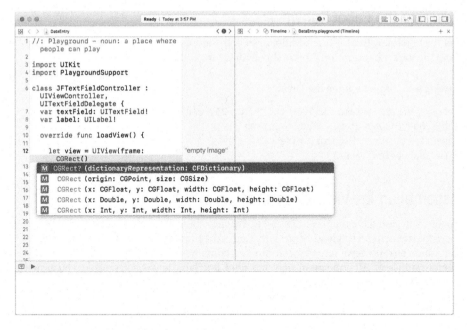

Figure 6-10. *Use the QuickType completions*

You can create the CGRect for the view with CGFloat, Double, or Int values. If you're not used to the QuickType keyboard, you'll soon find it's a big time saver (see Chapter 5 for more on that). It can also be a source of new ideas of how you can write code. For instance, in this case, Int values work perfectly well.

Creating the Text Field Subview

Listing 6-5 shows the text field implementation. It's almost exactly the same as what you have seen before: the view is created with its frame, its background color is set, and it's added to the main view (called view).

Listing 6-5. Implementing the Text Field

```
textField = UITextField (frame: CGRect (x: 5, y: 5, width: 100, height: 15))
textField.backgroundColor = UIColor.white
view.addSubview (textField)
```

Creating the Label Subview

For the label view there is one additional step: the text color is set to white so it stands out from the darker background. This is shown in Listing 6-6.

Listing 6-6. Implementing the Label

```
label = UILabel(frame: CGRect (x: 5, y: 25, width: 100, height: 15))
label.backgroundColor = UIColor.brown
label.textColor = UIColor.white
view.addSubview(label)
```

Assembling the View Controller

Finally, you assign the main view (view) to the view controller's view property. Each view controller has a single view property that is the primary view that it controls. That view often has subviews, and in fact it can be a container view whose purpose is only to contain subviews. After the main view, text field, and label have been created, you assign the main view (view) that you have created to the view controller's view:

```
self.view = view
```

Managing Text Fields

Cocoa and Cocoa Touch use the target-action design pattern extensively. It's a very simple idea that relies on the basic structure of Cocoa and its messaging structure. User interface objects typically use target-action whether or not you notice it (with storyboards, for example, the underpinnings are behind what you draw in a storyboard's graphical user interface).

The idea is that for a user interface control, when a certain action occurs send a message to a target and specify what action that target should take. In the case of an interface element like a text field, you set up the target and the action it should take with addTarget, a method of UIControl that includes buttons and sliders. addTarget's signature is addTarget(_:action:for:).

Here's the line of code you need to add to loadView():

```
textField.addTarget (self, action: #selector(updateText),
    for: UIControlEvents.editingChanged)
```

This method prepares the target-action design pattern for use:

- The first parameter is the target: in this case, the target is self— the view controller in which this line of code occurs. (Using self as the target is very common.)

- The action that's sent to the target (self) is to run the updateText method. This method is declared in the view controller, as you'll see in the next section.

- The condition for which the target-action will be triggered is specified by the `for:` parameter. In this case, it is `UIControlEvents.editingChanged`, which is a constant declared in the `UIControlEvents` struct.

Updating the Text

Once you have set up the target-action design pattern as shown here, you only need to implement that `updateText` method that will be called when a `UIControlEvents.editingChanged` message is received by the view controller. Remember that the view controller has references to both the text field and the label so it can pick up the text property of the text field and set its value to the label's text property. Listing 6-7 shows the code.

Listing 6-7. Updating the text label from the text field

```
func updateText () {
  self.label.text = textField.text
}
```

Finishing Up the View Controller

At the end of the view controller's code is a line that invokes `updateText` during `loadView`. This has the result of setting the value of `label` to the text in `textField`. Because `textField` was just created, that value is blank, which is what you want.

Finally, you create an instance of `JFTextFieldController` and assign it to the live view of the current page. Listing 6-8 shows the completed code.

Listing 6-8. Interactive Playground Code

```
/*:
  # Interactive Playground
  * DataEntry
  */

import UIKit
import PlaygroundSupport

class JFTextFieldController : UIViewController, UITextFieldDelegate {
  var textField: UITextField!
  var label: UILabel!

  override func loadView() {

    let view = UIView(frame: CGRect(x: 50, y: 50, width: 100, height: 100))
    view.backgroundColor = UIColor.cyan
```

```
    textField = UITextField (frame: CGRect (x: 5, y: 5, width: 100, height: 15))
    textField.backgroundColor = UIColor.white
    view.addSubview (textField)

    label = UILabel(frame: CGRect (x: 5, y: 25, width: 100, height: 15))
    label.backgroundColor = UIColor.brown
    label.textColor = UIColor.white
    view.addSubview(label)

    self.view = view

    textField.addTarget (self, action: #selector(updateText),
      for: UIControlEvents.editingChanged)

    updateText()
  }

  func updateText () {
    self.label.text = textField.text
  }
}

PlaygroundPage.current.liveView = JFTextFieldController()
```

Trying Out the Playground

You can try out the playground, as shown in Figure 6-11.

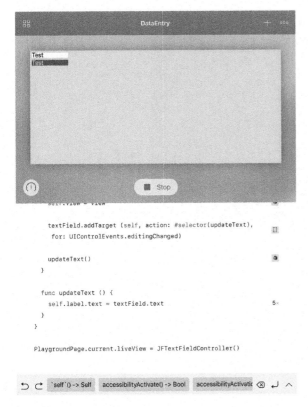

Figure 6-11. *Try out the playground*

Exploring the Playground

As your playground is running, you can examine what's happening. For example, as Figure 6-12 shows, you can tap the code to bring up a menu of choices. Note the disclosure triangles to the right of each property that is in play at the moment.

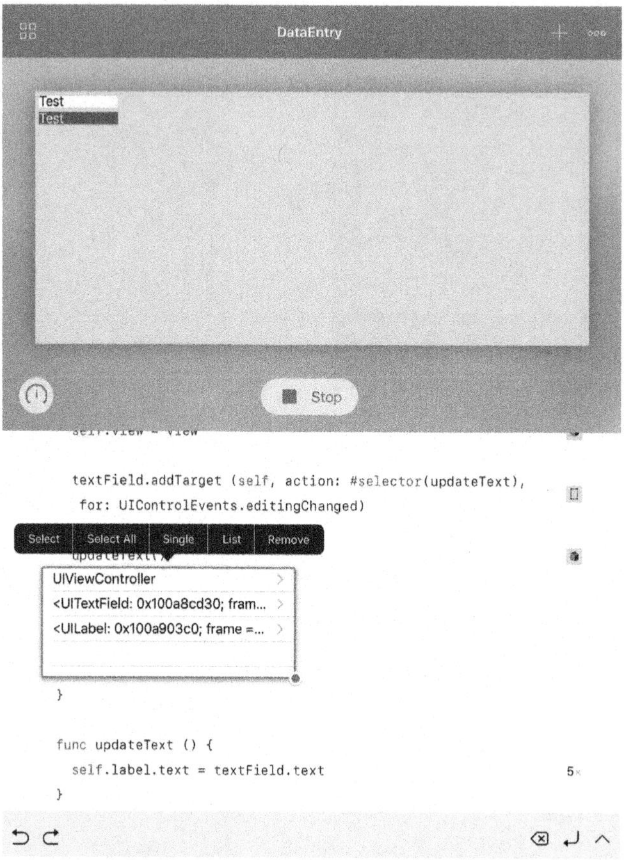

Figure 6-12. *Explore the properties as the playground runs*

Tap a disclosure triangle to see its runtime values, as shown in Figure 6-9. For example, tapping the view controller itself (such as the code that is the invocation of updateText), you will see that the UIViewController is a descendent of UIResponder, which in turn has its own disclosure triangle (shown in Figure 6-10).

You could continue drilling down to see any of the properties. At any level, you can stop drilling down and go back, as shown in Figure 6-13. You can then explore another part of the hierarchy, as you can see in Figure 6-14, where the label is explored. You see its property, the only one it has assigned at this point: the color. And in the playground's view, you see that color as it is (the actual color).

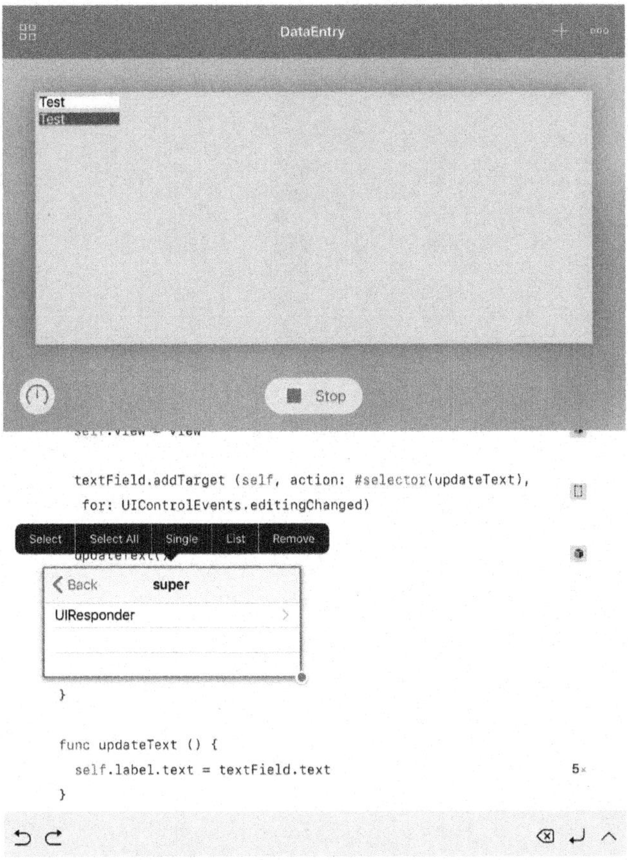

Figure 6-13. *Use the back arrow to back out of data for a given property*

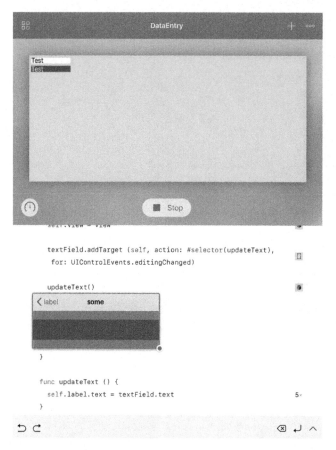

Figure 6-14. *Explore other parts of the playground's data structure*

Summary

In this chapter, you saw how to create interactive playgrounds in several ways. You can use the timeline to explore what is happening as the playground runs. You can build a playground that is subtantially more sophisticated so that users can enter data and see it in a text field or label. This interface uses the interface elements you will use in apps and other playgrounds, rather than the default Swift playground interfaces.

CHAPTER 7

Adding Resources and Source Code to Playgrounds

When you create a playground—either on a Mac with Xcode or using Playgrounds on an iPad—you can start writing your code right away. You can use import to bring in modules large and small, including ones that are focused on specific tasks such as managing audio or video or even playgrounds themselves (with PlaygroundSupport). You can control what parts of your code are visible in a playground by using markup commands such as //#-editable-code and //#-end-editable-code (see Chapters 4 and 6 for examples).

Playgrounds are actually packages of files that can include resources (most commonly images) and additional code. This chapter shows you how to add resources and source code to your playgrounds as well as how to explore playgrounds (including the Apple playgrounds) to see how things are done.

■ **Note**   Playgrounds can be much more complex than just the packages of files that you see in this chapter. You can assemble playgrounds into *playground books*. You'll see an example of that in Chapter 9.

Looking Inside a Playground

You can create a playground on a Mac with Xcode (a free download from http:// developer.apple.com or the Mac App Store) or on an iPad with the Playgrounds app. The playgrounds are transferable from one environment to the other, or you can save them to iCloud Drive or Dropbox so that you can access them from either place.

■ **Note**   In the figures in this chapter, you'll see both Playgrounds and Xcode. As files are moved back and forth, you can either share them or copy them to new versions. The figures in this chapter reflect the fact that many are copied. As you work on your own projects, you may prefer to share files because it's more straightforward. In preparing the screenshots in this book, copying them has been easier, so ignore the integers appended to playground titles.

A playground is actually a package of files that contain the components for a playground. You can look inside a playground on Xcode or Playgrounds. You see a bit more of the file structure when using Xcode and the Finder, so that way of exploring a playground is shown first in this section, but then you'll see how to look at the same playground and its files using Playgrounds on iPad.

The playground we'll explore is a very basic one called ExpandingPlaygrounds. You can create it either on macOS or an iPad. It has a title and subtitle—you can see the raw markup code in Figure 7-1 on macOS and rendered markup in Figure 7-2.

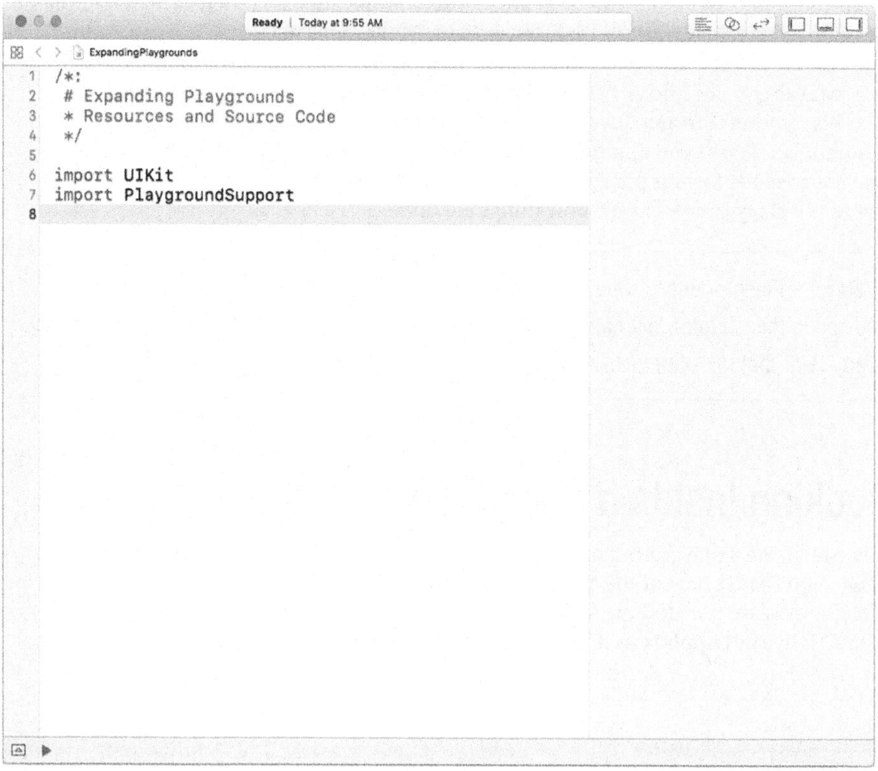

Figure 7-1. Raw markup for ExpandingPlaygrounds

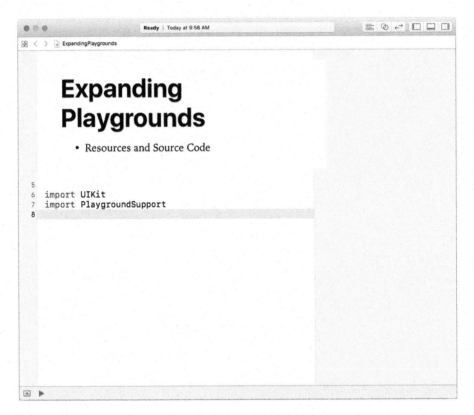

Figure 7-2. *Rendered markup for ExpandingPlaygrounds*

Exploring a Playground in the Finder (macOS)

Using the Finder in macOS, locate the playground you have created, as shown in Figure 7-3.

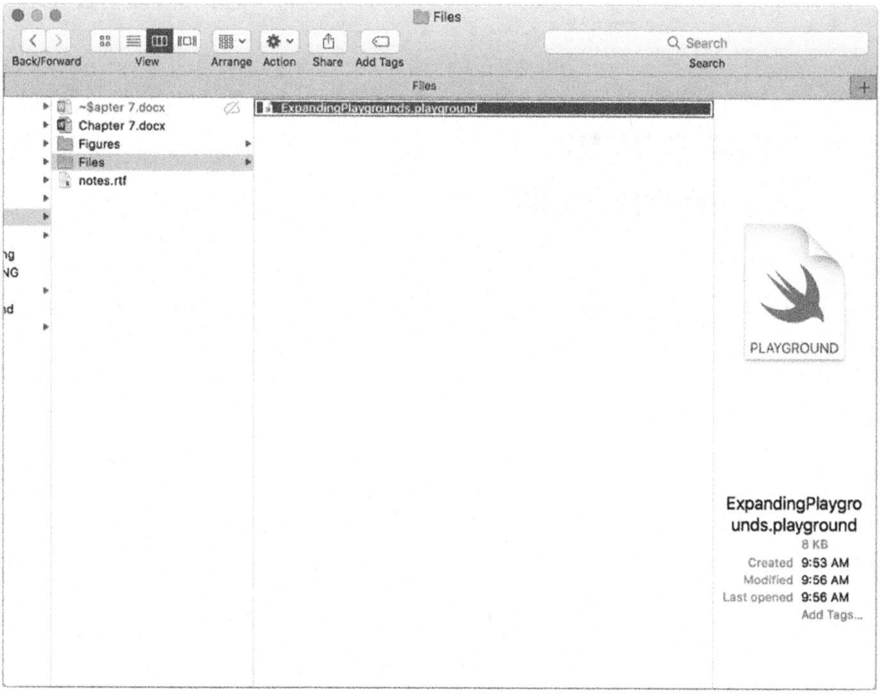

Figure 7-3. ExpandingPlaygrounds in the Finder on macOS

If you double-click the playground file, it will open in Xcode as a playground on macOS. But because it's a package, you can open the package itself to see the internal files. Control-clicking the playground file will show the shortcut menu in Figure 7-4.

■ **Note** As with most shortcut menus, you'll see the available menu commands for the selected file. This means that the specific commands toward the bottom of the shortcut menu may be different on your Mac, but Show Package Contents at the top should be in the shortcut menu.

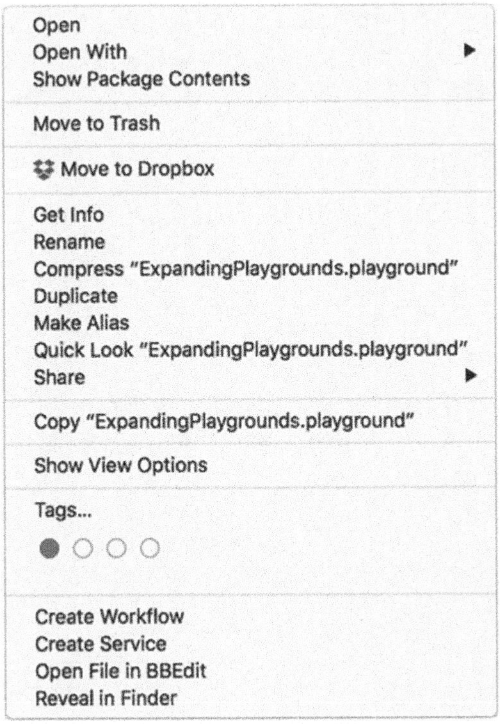

Open
Open With   ▶
Show Package Contents

Move to Trash

♻ Move to Dropbox

Get Info
Rename
Compress "ExpandingPlaygrounds.playground"
Duplicate
Make Alias
Quick Look "ExpandingPlaygrounds.playground"
Share   ▶

Copy "ExpandingPlaygrounds.playground"

Show View Options

Tags...
● ○ ○ ○

Create Workflow
Create Service
Open File in BBEdit
Reveal in Finder

Figure 7-4. *Use Control-click on macOS to open the playground's package*

Choose Show Package Contents to open the package in its own Finder window, as shown in Figure 7-5.

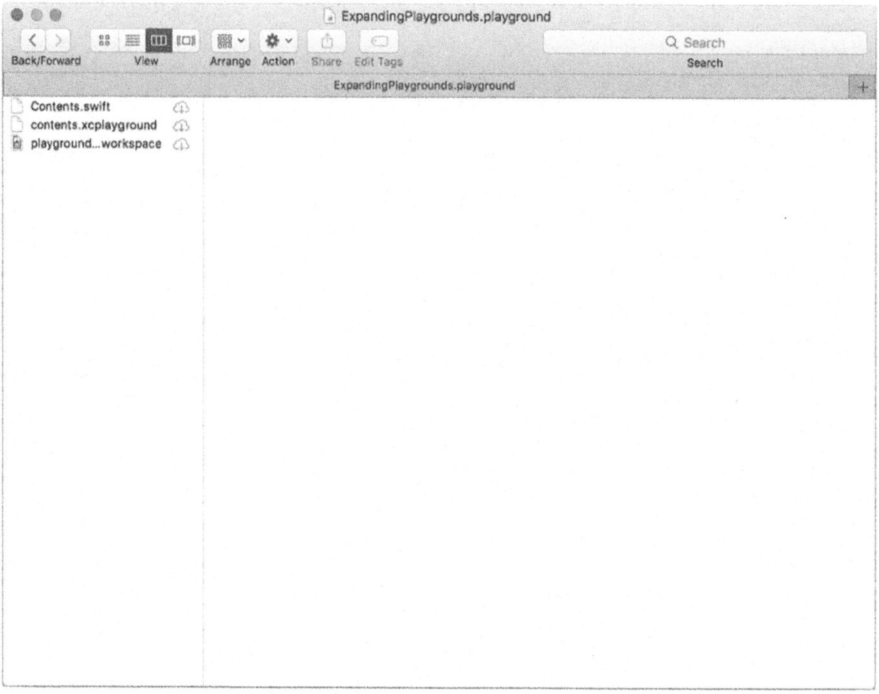

Figure 7-5. *Look inside the playground's package*

You will see the three basic playground files: Contents.swift, contents.xcplayground, and playground.workspace. You may also see two folders, Resources and Sources, which I describe after I talk about the three basic files.

Contents.swift

This is the basic playground file, shown in Figure 7-6; compare it to Figure 7-1. This is where the file shown in Figure 7-1 is located on disk. Resist the temptation to edit it inside the package—edit it with Xcode or with Playgrounds. (This will become more important as your playgrounds get bigger and more complex—see Chapter 9 for more details.)

Figure 7-6. *Look inside Contents.swift*

contents.xcplayground

contents.xcplayground is the basic directory of your playground and its files. Right now, there's only one file involved, but the playground may well grow. You can't open contents.xcplayground directly from the Finder, but you can open it with an editor such as BBEdit from the shortcut menu. (The comment about not editing these files directly definitely applies to this file. Look but don't edit!)

If you open this file, you'll see that it's an XML file. Listing 7-1 shows the code for this file that is in ExpandingPlaygrounds.

Listing 7-1. contents.xcplayground

```
<?xml version="1.0" encoding="UTF-8" standalone="yes"?>
<playground version='5.0' target-platform='ios' display-mode='rendered'>
  <timeline fileName='timeline.xctimeline'/>
</playground>
```

playground.workspace

Finally, playground.workspace is a typical Xcode workspace. (There's more on Xcode workspaces in the Xcode documentation, but you don't need to worry about it at this point—or possibly ever.) Because the package itself has your playground name in its title, the name of the workspace is constant: it's called playground.workspace even though in this case it's inside a playground called ExpandingPlaygrounds.

Exploring a Playground in Playgrounds (iOS)

You can open the same playground in Playgrounds on an iPad, or you can construct it from scratch in Playgrounds (and perhaps later you can open it on macOS in Xcode). Figure 7-7 shows the playground in Playgrounds.

ExpandingPlaygrounds 1

```
/*:
 # Expanding Playgrounds
 * Resources and Source Code
 */

import UIKit
import PlaygroundSupport
```

 Run My Code

Figure 7-7. ExpandingPlaygrounds in Playgrounds on iPad

Use the three dots at the top right of the Playgrounds view to open the Tools popover, as shown in Figure 7-8. You can use a variety of options to share your playground, such as taking a picture, creating a PDF, recording it, or broadcasting it using a live streaming app from the App Store (you'll find a link to those under the Broadcast Live tool item).

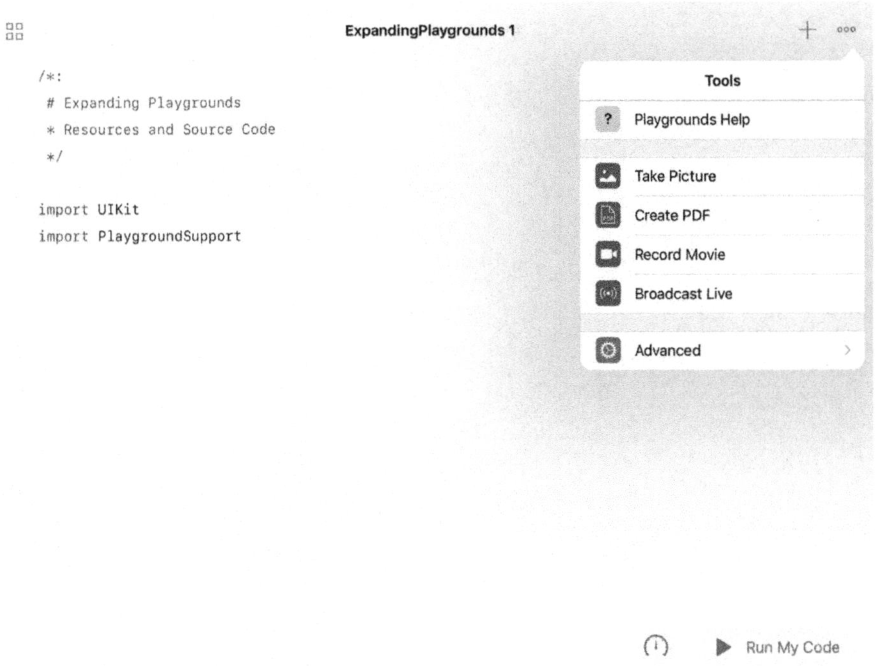

Figure 7-8. *Tools popover in Playgrounds on iPad*

To look inside the playground, tap Advanced at the bottom of the popover. You will start to explore the files inside the playground, as shown in Figure 7-9.

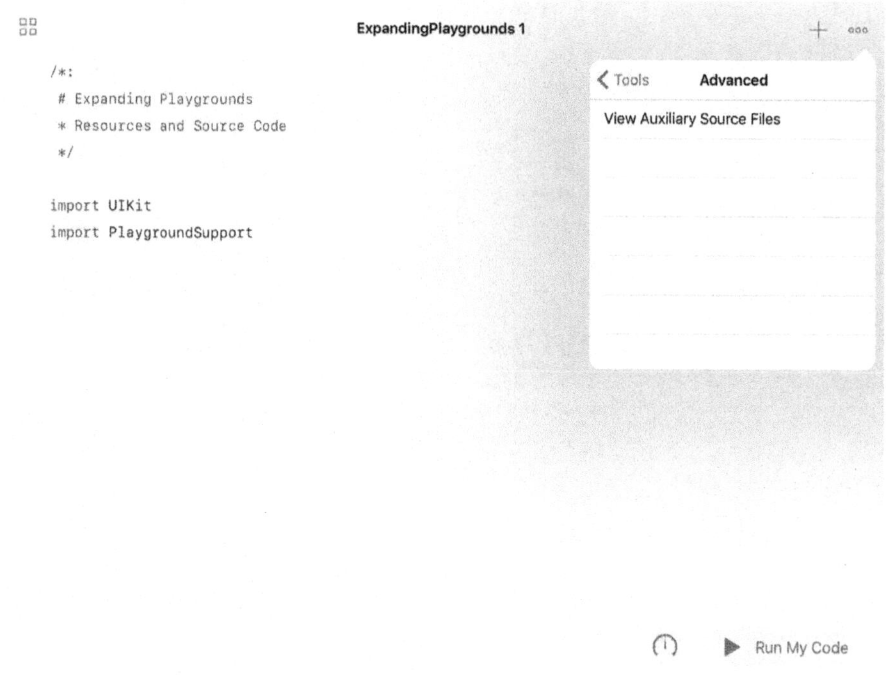

```
/*:
  # Expanding Playgrounds
  * Resources and Source Code
*/


import UIKit
import PlaygroundSupport
```

ExpandingPlaygrounds 1

‹ Tools   **Advanced**

View Auxiliary Source Files

Run My Code

Figure 7-9. *Exploring advanced tools in Playgrounds*

Tap View Auxiliary Source Files to delve into the playground, as you can see in Figure 7-10.

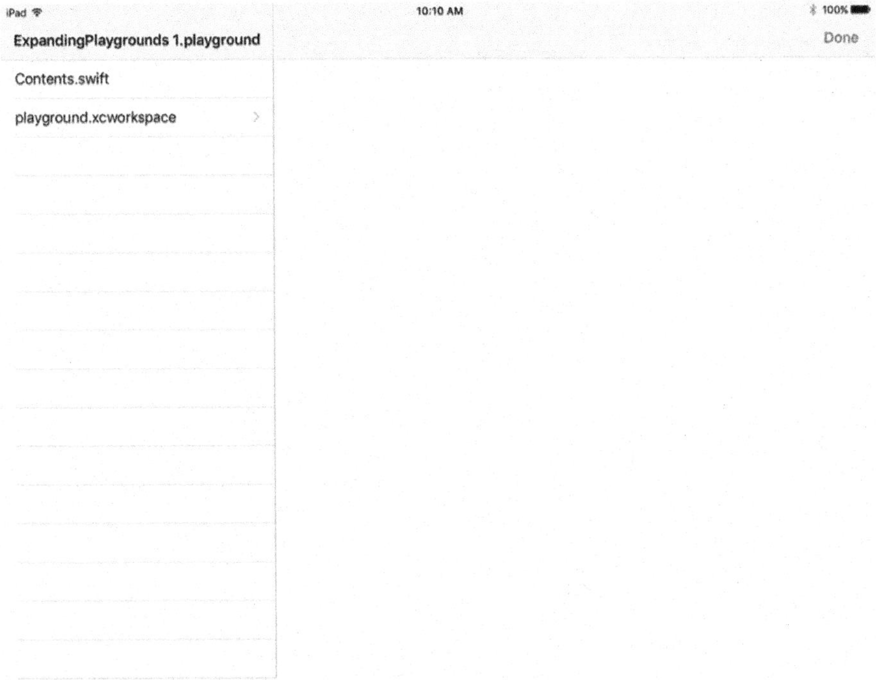

Figure 7-10. *Looking at auxiliary source files*

You're back to the playground package you saw back in Figure 7-5.

■ **Note**   There may be other files or directories that are shown at this point. Unless you've been changing the inside of the playground, don't worry about them. contents.xcplayground shown in Listing 7-1 may not be shown. Resources and Sources folders may appear (covered in the following sections).

If you have any doubts, tap Contents.swift; the result is shown in Figure 7-11.

Figure 7-11. *Look inside Contents.swift*

Adding Resources to a Playground

You can add resources to a playground just by selecting them or dragging them into the playground in Playgrounds (iOS) or in Xcode (macOS—see Figure 7-12) as part of a statement, such as this one:

```
let myImage =
```

■ **Note**   You can use Xcode on macOS or Playgrounds on iOS as you switch back and forth to a shared file (perhaps using iCloud Drive). There is no single way to integrate resources into your playgrounds, so this section moves back and forth to show the various steps you can take on both platforms.

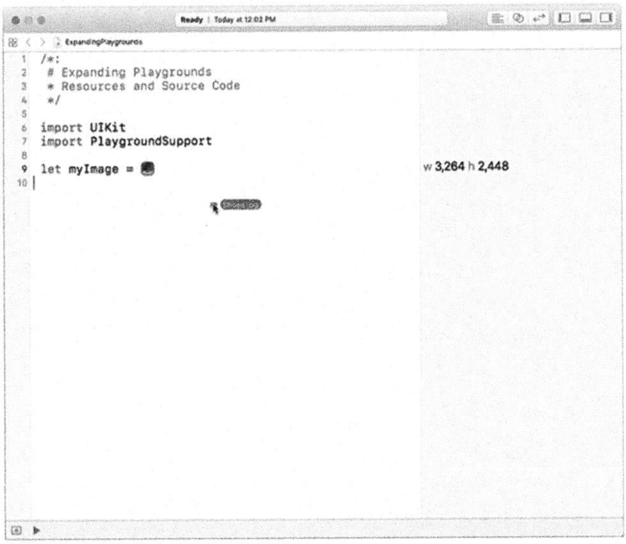

Figure 7-12. *Drag an image file on macOS*

The completed line of code is shown in Figure 7-13.

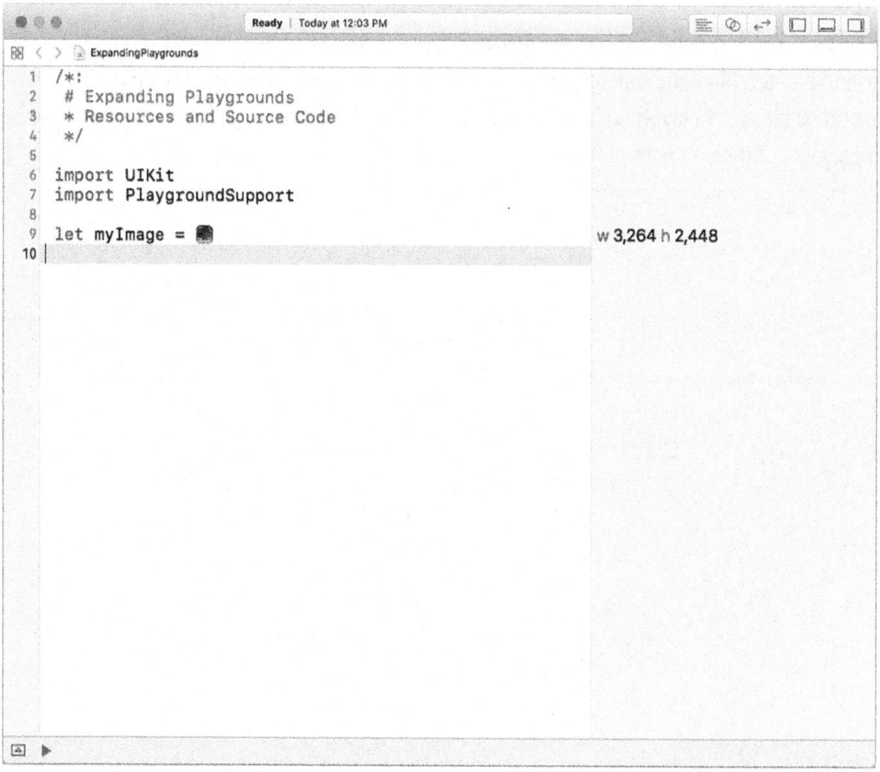

Figure 7-13. *The image is inserted into the code*

Behind the scenes, if you look at the package you'll see that now there is a Resources folder that may not have been there before. Inside it, you'll find the image file that you just dropped into the playground, as shown in Figure 7-14 (this is in Xcode on macOS).

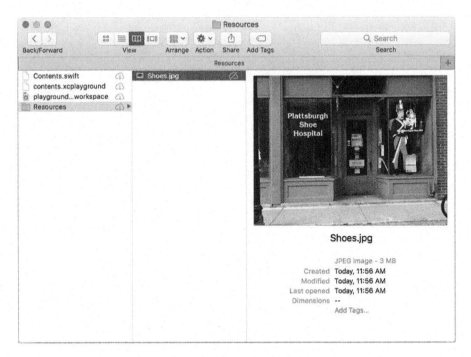

Figure 7-14. *The image drag is completed and it is placed in Resources*

The Resources folder is also now present in Playgrounds on iOS, as you can see in Figure 7-15.

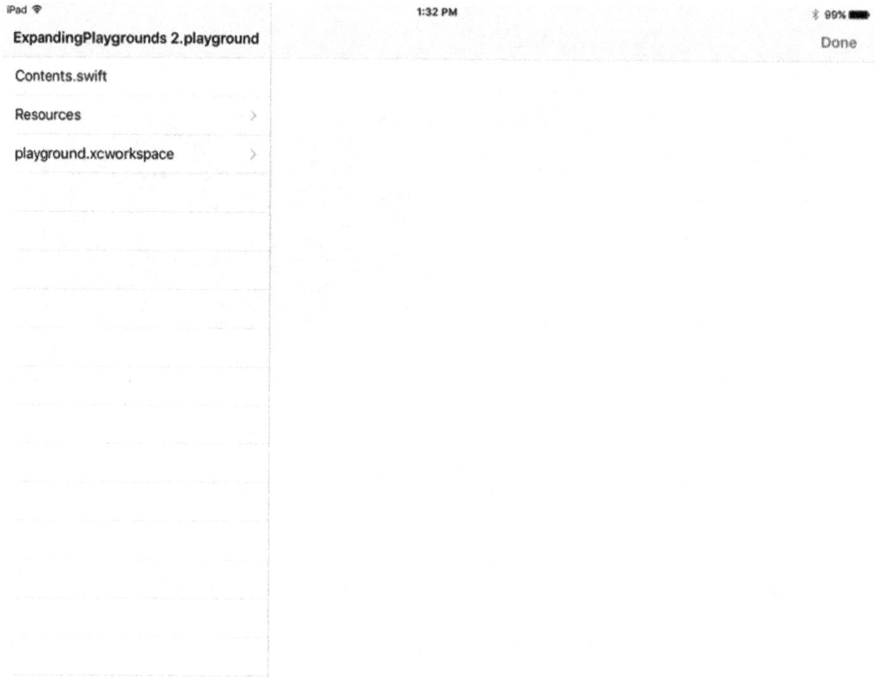

Figure 7-15. *Resources folder is added if necessary*

In Playgrounds on iOS, you don't drag files into playgrounds (dragging files is a macOS technique). Instead, to add a file, double-tap an image placeholder or any other place where an image may be placed.

In the Shortcut Bar at the bottom of the Playgrounds view in Figure 7-16, you'll see that in the context of the code, you can choose to complete the replacement statement with (from left to right) a number, string, Boolean value, shape, or picture, as well as an array, dictionary, tuple, or nil.

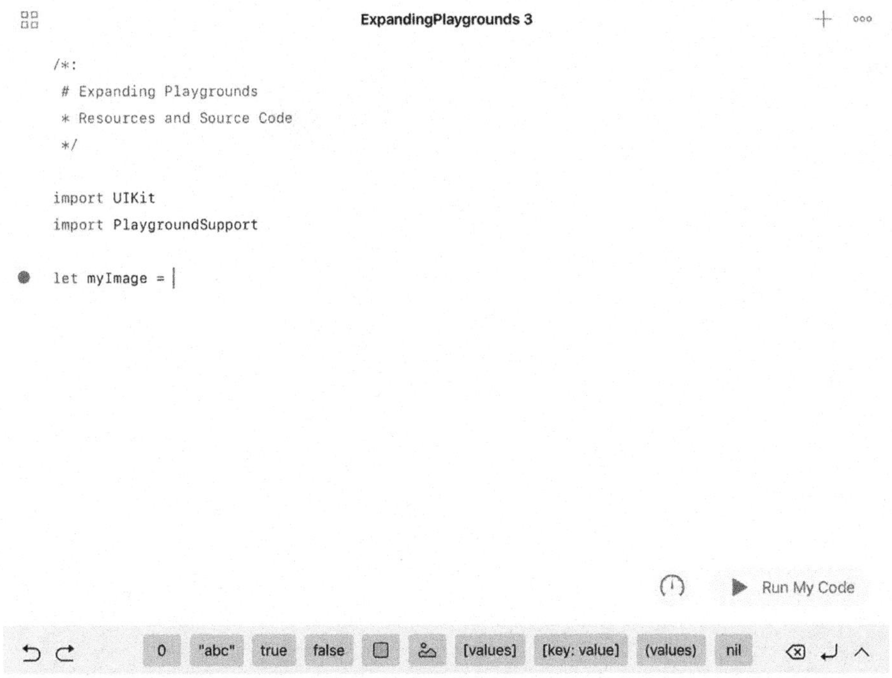

```
/*:
 # Expanding Playgrounds
 * Resources and Source Code
 */

import UIKit
import PlaygroundSupport

let myImage = |
```

Figure 7-16. *The Shortcut Bar lets you insert a picture*

The picture button on the Shortcut Bar (the sun/moon and mountain button) opens the popover shown in Figure 7-17. The popover lets you select from the three types of resources that can be inserted into a playground. The segmented control at the top shows them (from left to right): code snippets, pictures, and documents.

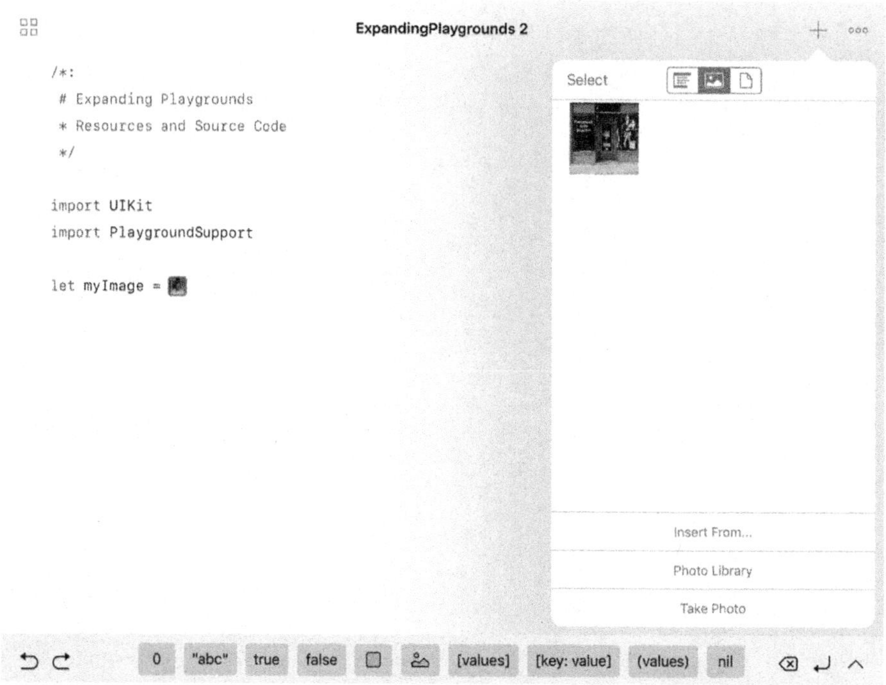

Figure 7-17. *Insert a picture from Resources*

When you have chosen (or taken a photo of) an image that you want to use, you can tap it to enlarge it and then tap Use in the top right of the view, as shown in Figure 7-18.

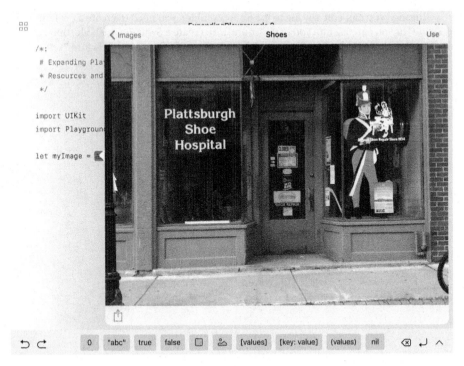

Figure 7-18. Use a photo

Adding Code to a Playground

In addition to adding resources, you can add code to a playground. This code is added to the Sources folder (you may need to create it) and is executed as your playground runs. You can add more than one file to the Sources folder. Place Swift code in the files that you want to reference in your playground. Code placed in the Sources folder runs faster than code in your playground, so you may want to do this for reasons of efficiency.

More common is using code in the Sources folder to provide behind-the-scenes features to your playground. The following are three common ways of using files in Sources. The first is demonstrated in this chapter; the second two are shown in Chapter 9:

- You can create a function in a file in the Sources folder so that you can use it in the playground. This is commonly used in training and education playgrounds, where the emphasis is on the overall view and the details of implementation for a function don't matter because the focus is on the big picture.

- You can create a class in a Sources file that you use in your playground as needed.

- You can create a constant or an enum to be used in various parts of your playground.

131

Although you can edit any file in the Sources folder, you need to create a Swift file in Xcode (or you can use one you have around). To create a Swift file in Xcode, open or create a playground in Xcode. Then use File ➤ New ➤ File, as shown in Figure 7-19.

Figure 7-19. *Create a Swift file in Xcode*

Click Next and continue to save the file wherever you want to. You can save it directly into the Sources folder of your playground or save it elsewhere and then drag it into the Sources folder of your playground.

You can also use the project navigator in Xcode to add a file. Open your playground in Xcode and show the project navigator at the left of the workspace window, as shown in Figure 7-20. (You use the navigator button at the top right of the workspace window or View ➤ Navigators ➤ Show Project Navigator to show the project navigator).

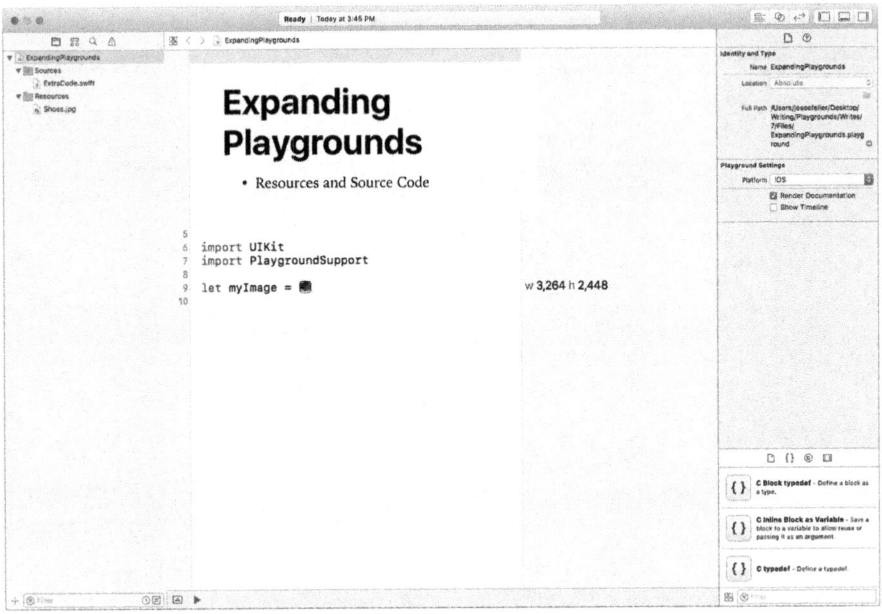

Figure 7-20. *Show the project navigator in Xcode on macOS*

Use the + at the bottom left of the project navigator to add a new file, as you can see in Figure 7-21.

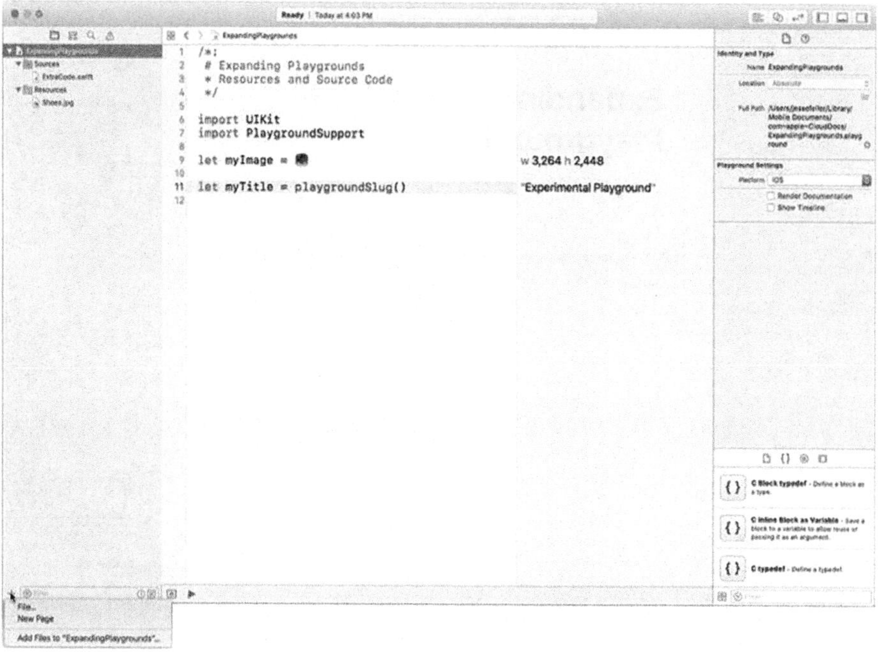

Figure 7-21. *Add a new file to your Xcode project*

In Figure 7-21, the new file is named ExtraCode.swift, but you can name it anything you want because the file name won't appear in the main playground. In Xcode, you can open the file from the project navigator and write a function or other code, as shown in Figure 7-22.

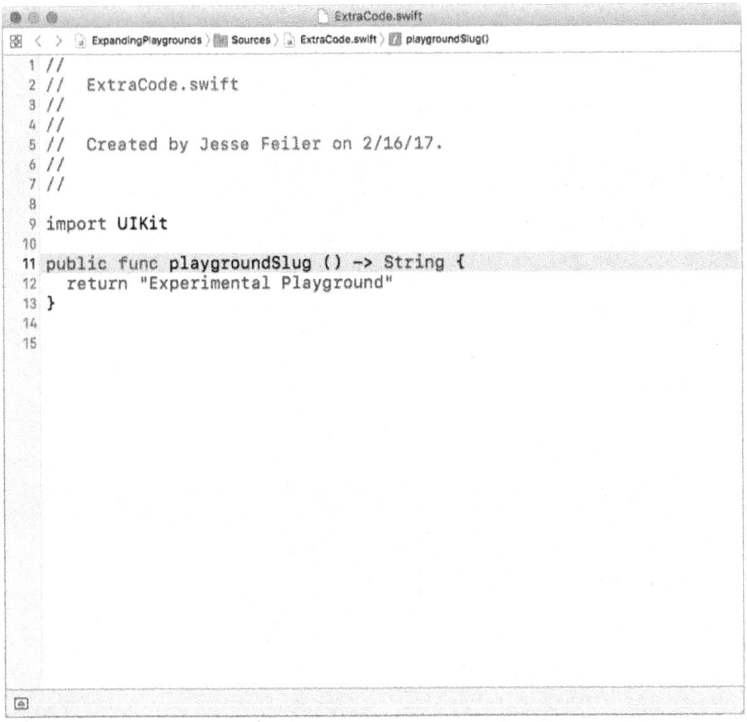

Figure 7-22. Open and edit the ExtraCode.swift file in Xcode

■ **Tip**   Make functions and classes in your added source files `public`. Also note that the blank file that is created for you will have an `import` statement—typically to import Foundation, Cocoa, or UIKit. Choose the lowest level you need. In other words, if you don't need the user interface, choose Foundation or Cocoa.

In Playgrounds on iOS, you can always use the three dots at the top right of the window to look inside the playground. At this point, you'll see more components, as shown in Figure 7-23.

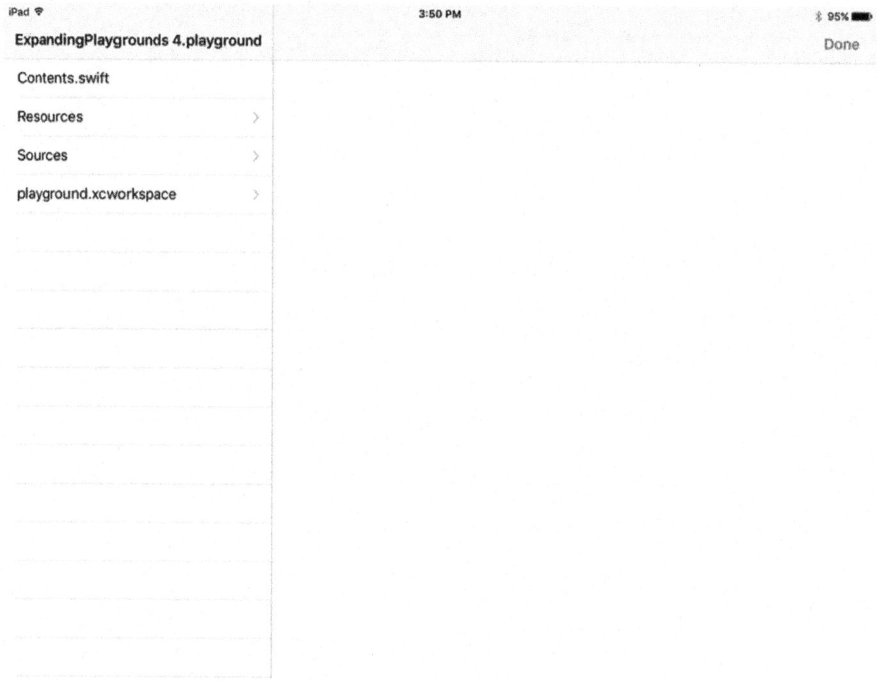

Figure 7-23. *Look inside your playground as you add more components*

You can drill down into the Sources folder; your new file is there, as you can see in Figure 7-24.

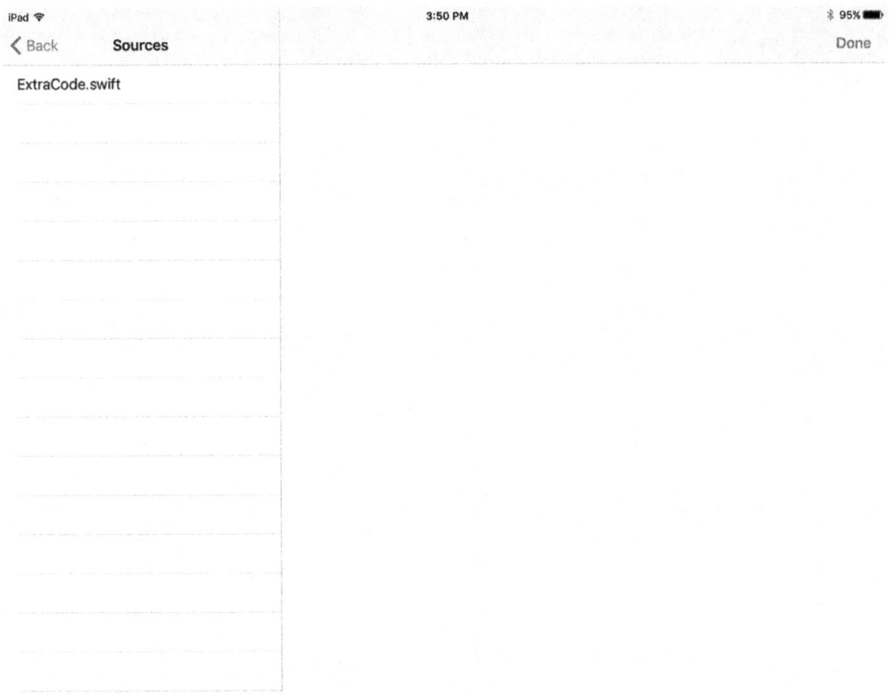

Figure 7-24. *Drill down to ExtraCode.swift*

Select ExtraCode.swift from Sources at the left, and you'll see your code, as shown in Figure 7-25. You can edit it either here in Playgrounds or in Xcode. Remember to either move the playground back and forth or work on the shared copy in iCloud Drive or Dropbox.

```
iPad ⚌                                    3:50 PM                              ⚌ 95% ▮▮▮
  ‹ Back      Sources                                                          Done

 ExtraCode.swift              //
                             //    ExtraCode.swift
                             //
                             //
                             //    Created by Jesse Feiler on 2/16/17.
                             //
                             //
                             import UIKit

                             public func playgroundSlug () -> String {
                                 return "Experimental Playground"
                             }
```

Figure 7-25. *View and edit your code in Xcode*

Once you have your code in the Sources folder, you can use its functions, classes, and other code in your main playground files. For example, you can use the playgroundSlug function to return a string to use in your playground. Do that in your main playground, as shown in Figure 7-26.

ExpandingPlaygrounds 4   + ∘∘∘

```
/*:
 # Expanding Playgrounds
 * Resources and Source Code
 */

import UIKit
import PlaygroundSupport

let myImage = 

let myTitle = playgroundSlug()
```

⊙   ▶ Run My Code

Figure 7-26. *Use the function from ExtraCode.swift in your playground*

As you're typing your code, you'll see that although `playgroundSlug` isn't visible, it's visible to QuickType—it's among the choices available as you type. This is shown in Figure 7-27.

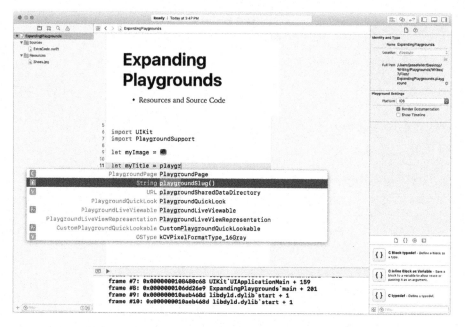

Figure 7-27. *QuickType can see your added code in Sources*

If you run the playground on Xcode, you'll see that the function is being called, as shown in Figure 7-28.

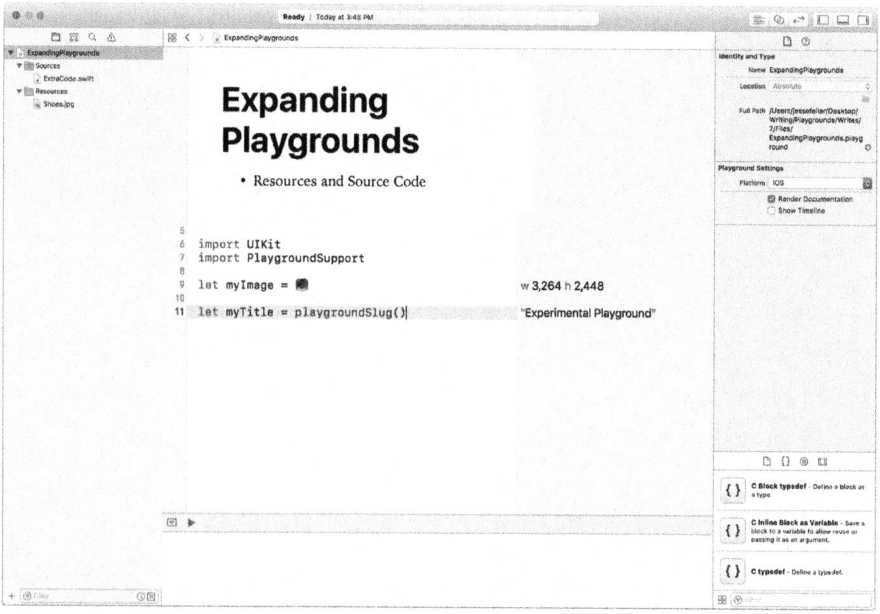

Figure 7-28. *The function in ExtraCode.swift is called from your playground*

In Playgrounds on your iPad, you'll see that it's also running there, as shown in Figure 7-29.

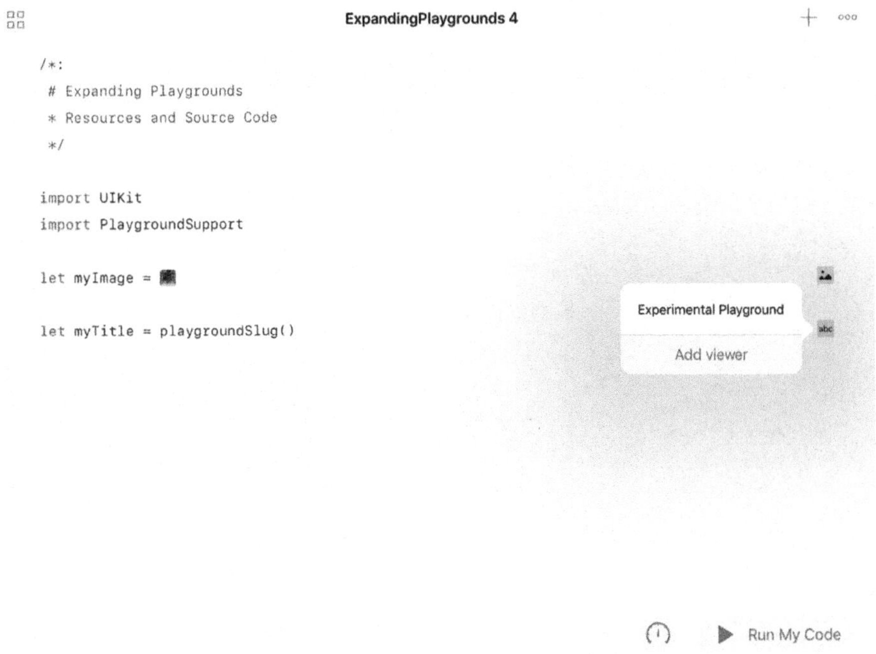

Figure 7-29. *The code is available on both macOS and iPad*

There's no visible reference to ExtraCode.swift, and the code that's in the function isn't shown at all. For teaching purposes, this can be great because you can focus on the flow of control in the playground and then drill down (if necessary) to the code in Sources.

Summary

This chapter showed how to add images or other resources to a playground as well as how to add code to a playground. Resources and source code are parts of the playground and are available to the main playground and to any other pages you might add to your playground. In Chapter 9 you'll see how to add new pages to your playground that use the added resources and code.

CHAPTER 8

■ ■ ■

Using Touch Gestures in Interactive Playgrounds

Chapter 6 explores interactivity in playgrounds for two major areas:

- Working with a playground live view and views that respond to device rotation

- Creating and using data entry fields

This chapter explores yet another aspect of interactive views: creating and using gesture recognizers so you can create playgrounds with objects that users can directly manipulate.

All of these examples use views inside a playground live view. In Cocoa and Cocoa Touch, views are not just displays of data—they also respond to events such as device rotation, along with touches in subclasses of UIView such as UIButton. Views are also movable and resizable when you add gesture recognizers to them.

Because both Chapter 6 and this chapter are based on views, you can mix and match the various code snippets you see in the examples. For example, you can create a view with subviews for display and data entry (as in Chapter 6) and then make it movable, as shown in this chapter.

That's not all. You can explore sample code on http://developer.apple.com such as UIKit Dynamics Catalog (https://developer.apple.com/library/content/samplecode/DynamicsCatalog/Introduction/Intro.html) to take advantage of built-in physics functionality that reflects gravity, collisions, and other real-world movement.

Adding gestures to your playgrounds can make them much more powerful and inviting for your users. For you, using playgrounds to explore the world of touch gestures is a great way to get a firsthand understanding of gestures. Until you actually use gestures and experiment with the code that backs them up, you don't get a good sense of what is going on. In part that's because gestures combine many different aspects of the user interface, so experimenting with gestures in code for an app can require a lot of preparation and setup. In a playground that you use for exploration, you can use stripped-down gestures to get a sense of the functionality and then go back to fully implement them in an app or playground for others.

© Jesse Feiler 2017

J. Feiler, *Exploring Swift Playgrounds*, DOI 10.1007/978-1-4842-2647-6_8

Understanding Gestures Using Playgrounds

Gestures entered the Mac world with the advent of trackpads on Macs (specifically the MacBook Air and models of MacBook Pro). As described in "Cocoa Event Handling Guide," https://developer.apple.com/library/content/documentation/Cocoa/ Conceptual/EventOverview/HandlingTouchEvents/HandlingTouchEvents.html, "...gesture events are a species of multitouch events because they're based on an interpretation of a sequence of touches. In other words, gestures are a series of multitouch events recognized by the trackpad as constituting a gesture." What is important is that they are *sequences* of more than one event. The sequence has a beginning and an end with its first and last event; the intermediate events may be of several types, but often they are of the same type. These intermediate events (such as moving your finger on the trackpad or device screen) continue as the gesture continues. Although each gesture has a start with a beginning event, it may not have an ending event because it may be cancelled. This is much more complex than a tap gesture, which consists of two events: touch down and touch up.

■ **Note**   This chapter is an introduction to help you get started with understanding and using gestures. There are many simplifications both in the structure of the playground and its functionality, but you should get a working gesture-recognizing playground that you can then enhance and customize for your own purposes.

Creating a Basic Gesture Playground in Xcode on macOS

In this section, you'll see how to build a playground with a basic gesture to get a feel for how gestures work. This will entail creating a new playground with a live view as a background and then creating a view that's inside the live view. That view will respond to gestures.

Creating a Playground with Live View

Begin by creating a basic playground with a live view, as shown in Figure 8-1, where the timeline is shown in the Assistant Editor. The code is shown in Listing 8-1.

■ **Note**   The background of mainView in Figure 8-1 and Listing 8-1 is set to brown to make it clearer in some of the figures of this chapter. It's better to set it to white as you work on this project, and that's how it is used in the later figures in this chapter. If you look very carefully at the timeline with a white mainView, you'll see that the background of the timeline is a very light gray, and the white mainView is visible as a separate view—but it's not easy to spot unless you're used to it, thus the much more visible brown in some of the figures in this chapter.

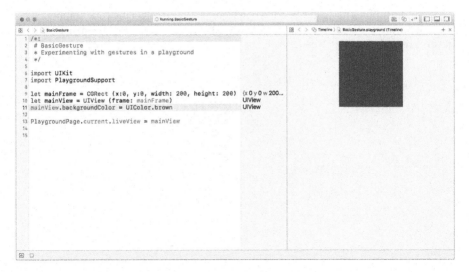

Figure 8-1. *Code for simple playground*

Listing 8-1. Creating a Simple Playground

```
/*:
 # BasicGesture
 * Experimenting with gestures in a playground
 */

import UIKit
import PlaygroundSupport

let mainFrame = CGRect (x:0, y:0, width: 200, height: 200)
let mainView = UIView (frame: mainFrame)
mainView.backgroundColor = UIColor.brown

PlaygroundPage.current.liveView = mainView
```

Create a GestureView Class

Create the inner view that will respond to gestures. To do so, you will need to create a subclass of UIView that responds to gestures. Thus, you need to create a new class (call it GestureView) which is a subclass of UIView, and you'll need to create an instance of GestureView that you add to mainView.

■ **Note**　This is not the only way to create a view that responds to gestures, but it's simple enough to get started.

145

Show the utilities navigator, as shown in Figure 8-2, and select the code snippet library at the lower right. In it, you'll find a Swift subclass snippet that you can use for the GestureView subclass of UIView.

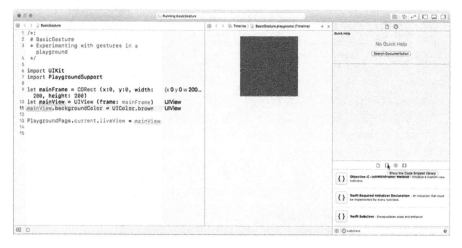

Figure 8-2. *Use a Swift subclass snippet*

For now, it makes sense to put the GestureView subclass at the top of your playground file, right after the import statements. (This choice is to keep your code organized—you'll move it after you've confirmed that your basic gesture is working.) Figure 8-3 shows the code snippet dragged into your playground.

Figure 8-3. *Add the snippet to your playground's code*

When you release the mouse button (or let up on the trackpad), the code snippet is inserted in your playground as you see in Figure 8-4.

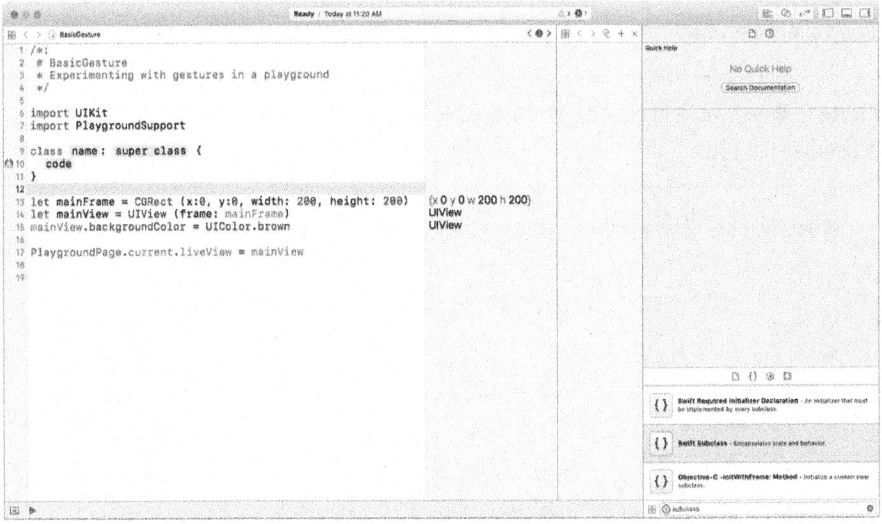

Figure 8-4. *Check the snippet once it's added to your code*

As with all code snippets, there are placeholders you have to fill in with actual code. If you try to build an app or playground with them in place, you'll get errors. In the case of the subclass snippet, you need to name the new subclass as well as its superclass. Then you need to add its code.

In the case of this new subclass, the first two substitutions are simple: the new subclass is GestureView, and the superclass is UIView, so you can type those in. Listing 8-2 shows your playground's code as it should be at this point. The results are shown in Figure 8-5.

Listing 8-2. Entering the Class Name and Superclass Name

```
/*:
 # BasicGesture
 * Experimenting with gestures in a playground
 */

import UIKit
import PlaygroundSupport

public class GestureView: UIView {

}
```

```
let mainFrame = CGRect (x:0, y:0, width: 200, height: 200)
let mainView = UIView (frame: mainFrame)
mainView.backgroundColor = UIColor.brown

PlaygroundPage.current.liveView = mainView
```

■ **Note**   When you add classes or functions to your class for a playground, they must be declared as `public`.

Make the new class public as you see in Figure 8-5.

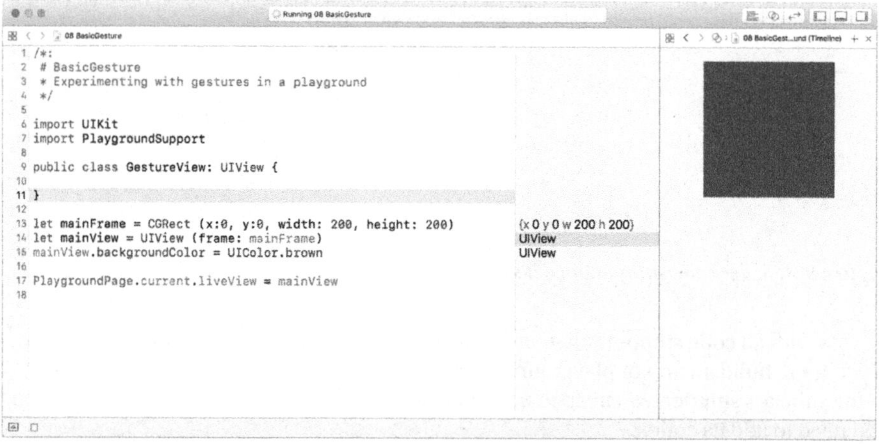

Figure 8-5. *Run the playground with the* `GestureView` *class in it (but not yet used)*

Once you see that the playground runs with the `GestureView` class (even though it's not used yet), it's a good time to change the `mainView` `backgroundColor` to white from brown. As noted previously, it will be a bit more difficult to see it, but you've now seen that the code is working, so that doesn't matter.

Creating an Instance of GestureView

Create an instance of `GestureView` and add it to your `mainView`. The code is the same as you've seen in similar cases—it's shown in Listing 8-3.

Listing 8-3. Creating a GestureView Instance

```
let innerFrame = CGRect (x:0, y:0, width: 200, height: 100)
let innerView = GestureRect (frame: innerFrame)
innerView.backgroundColor = UIColor.blue

mainView.addSubview(innerView)
```

Adding a Gesture to GestureView

With no gestures in place, when you look at the view in the timeline, it just sits there. Tap it or click it and nothing happens. The first gesture we'll explore will let you move it is called a *pan* gesture. You tap or click a view and drag it to a new position. Remember, gestures consist of a collection of multitouch events, so there will be several such events in the pan gesture, but you don't have to worry about that; Cocoa Touch will put the events together into a gesture for you.

To add a gesture to your view, you need to make five changes to the GestureView class. They are summarized here and shown in detail after the summary:

- Add an override of the init function for your class so you can use it to implement the gesture recognizer in the next step.

- You will need to add a required init function once you have added your init override, but the code need not be customized beyond the code shown in this section.

- Create a gesture recognizer to do just that—put the events together into a gesture. Your gesture recognizer in this case will be an instance of UIPanGestureRecognizer. (You'll see how to use a different gesture recognizer—UITapGestureRecognizer—later in this chapter.)

- Create the gesture recognizer in the UIView subclass init function and store it in a property of the class instance, as you will see in this section.

- Create a function to handle the pan gesture once it's recognized and while it continues.

The gesture recognizer will use the function that handles the pan gesture, so until you have the gesture recognizer and the gesture handler implemented, you can't test your code. Fortunately, there are only a few lines to test. They are shown in Listing 8-4. Create an override of the init function in your GestureView class.

Listing 8-4. Adding an init Function

```
override public init (frame: CGRect) {
  super.init(frame: frame)

  let panRecognizer = UIPanGestureRecognizer
    (target: self, action: #selector(pan(sender:)))
  addGestureRecognizer(panRecognizer)
}
```

Listing 8-4 creates the gesture recognizer and sets it up to notify itself (that is, the GestureView instance) and to use the pan gesture handler, which you'll write in the next step. Note that the syntax for selectors has changed with Swift 3, so this code may look a bit different from what you're used to. The main difference is that you no longer use quotes around a function name.

Once you add your override of init, you need to add the override of the required init, as shown in Listing 8-5. You normally use this code as-is.

Listing 8-5. Add the Required init

```
required public init?(coder aDecoder: NSCoder) {
  fatalError("init(coder:) has not been implemented")
}
```

Implement the gesture handler with the code in Listing 8-6.

Listing 8-6. Implement the pan Function

```
public func pan (sender: UIPanGestureRecognizer) {
  self.superview?.bringSubview (toFront: self)
  let translation = sender.translation (in: self.superview)
  sender.view!.center = CGPoint (
    x: sender.view!.center.x + translation.x,
    y: sender.view!.center.y + translation.y)
  sender.setTranslation(CGPoint (x:0, y:0), in: self.superview)
}
```

You may be able to use this code without any alteration in your own app or playground (if you do, use the version at the end of this chapter which incorporates a few additions). The code does the following:

- It asks the superview to bring the view (GestureView, in this case) to the front. Only a superview can bring a subview forward or move it in most cases.

- It stores the translation property of sender in a local variable called translation. translation is a CGPoint representing where the new panned location is. With the superview passed in, that panned location is in the superview's coordinates. Remember that the pan gesture recognizer is called repeatedly during the pan (that is, during the move) of a view.

- The handler then sets the center of the GestureView to the translated location.

- Finally, the translation is reset to 0, 0 in the superview's coordinates, reflecting the new position. If you don't do this, the view will move erratically as you drag it.

Adding Another GestureView

You add another GestureView with the code in Listing 8-7 so that you can try moving two views around. It's the same code you've used before, but the names of the frame and the view are changed, and the background color is changed, as well as the location of the view.

Listing 8-7. Add innerView2

```
let innerFrame2 = CGRect (x:20, y:20, width: 50, height: 50)
let innerView2 = GestureView (frame: innerFrame2)
innerView2.backgroundColor = UIColor.green
mainView.addSubview(innerView2)
```

Finishing Up

If all has gone well, you should have a green view that looks just like a UIView in your timeline, as shown in Figure 8-6.

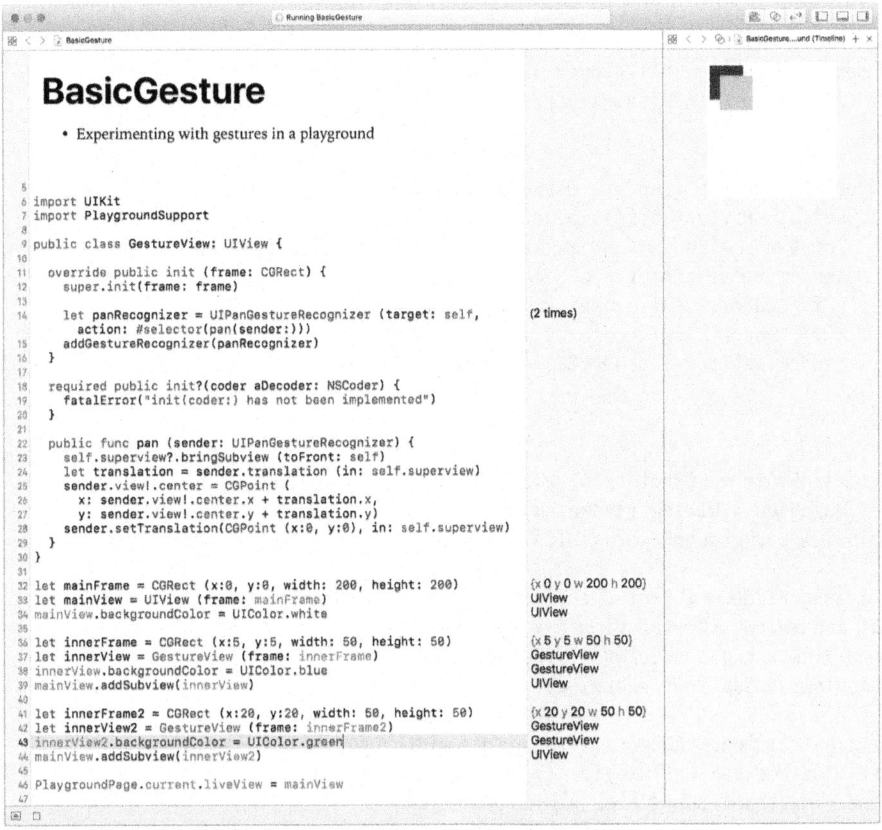

Figure 8-6. Test your code with the second GestureView

The full code for the playground is shown in Listing 8-8.

Listing 8-8. Complete Code for the Playground

```
import UIKit
import PlaygroundSupport

public class GestureView: UIView {

  override public init (frame: CGRect) {
    super.init(frame: frame)

    let panRecognizer = UIPanGestureRecognizer (target: self,
      action: #selector(pan(sender:)))
    addGestureRecognizer(panRecognizer)
  }

  required public init?(coder aDecoder: NSCoder) {
    fatalError("init(coder:) has not been implemented")
  }

  public func pan (sender: UIPanGestureRecognizer) {
    self.superview?.bringSubview (toFront: self)
    let translation = sender.translation (in: self.superview)
    sender.view!.center = CGPoint (
      x: sender.view!.center.x + translation.x,
      y: sender.view!.center.y + translation.y)
    sender.setTranslation(CGPoint (x:0, y:0), in: self.superview)
  }
}

let mainFrame = CGRect (x:0, y:0, width: 200, height: 200)
let mainView = UIView (frame: mainFrame)
mainView.backgroundColor = UIColor.white

let innerFrame = CGRect (x:5, y:5, width: 50, height: 50)
let innerView = GestureView (frame: innerFrame)
innerView.backgroundColor = UIColor.blue
mainView.addSubview(innerView)

let innerFrame2 = CGRect (x:20, y:20, width: 50, height: 50)
let innerView2 = GestureView (frame: innerFrame2)
innerView2.backgroundColor = UIColor.green
mainView.addSubview(innerView2)

PlaygroundPage.current.liveView = mainView
```

Creating a Basic Gesture Playground in Playgrounds on iPad

You can repeat the steps to create a basic gesture playground with Playgrounds on iPad. The few differences you'll see along the way are highlighted in this section. Start by creating a new playground from the blank template you see when you tap the + in the top left of the screen and choose Create Playground, as shown in Figure 8-7.

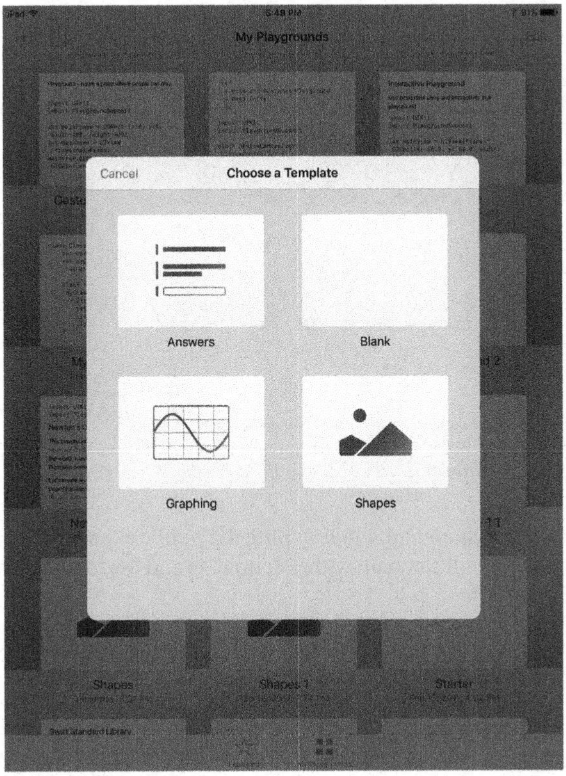

Figure 8-7. *Create a new playground in Playgrounds for iPad*

In the blank playground you see, you can start to type your code (if you want to refer to Listing 8-8, that may help you).

To begin creating your playground in a blank template, you'll need to start with the import statements. They're not shown in the Shortcut Bar, so show the keyboard with the button at the bottom right of the playground view, and start typing import, as shown in Figure 8-8. As soon as you have the first few characters typed, the Shortcut Bar will be able to guide you along.

Figure 8-8. *Start to create a new playground on iPad*

As soon as you finish with the `import` statements, start typing the public class declaration. Once again, the Shortcut Bar will catch up with you quickly and begin to offer you more help, as you can see in Figure 8-9.

Figure 8-9. *The Shortcut Bar helps you out*

As is always the case with the Shortcut Bar, it can't offer you suggestions when you create a new symbol of any kind because you could name it anything. Thus, in Figure 8-10, you will have to type GestureView without any prompting. You also will need to provide the colon and the superclass (UIView) name because these can't be predicted.

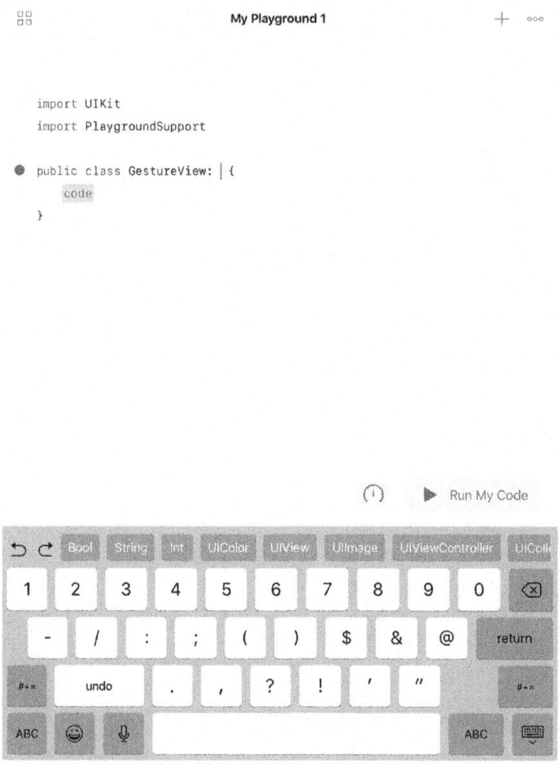

My Playground 1   +   ∘∘∘

```
import UIKit
import PlaygroundSupport

public class GestureView: | {
    code
}
```

⟲   ▶ Run My Code

Figure 8-10. *Type* `GestureView`

At this point, either type the code from Listing 8-8 or copy and paste it from the playground you created on Xcode (if you worked through that section—if you didn't, refer to the section "Creating a Basic Gesture Playground in Xcode on macOS," earlier in this chapter).

Whichever way you proceed, you should now have the playground shown in Figure 8-11.

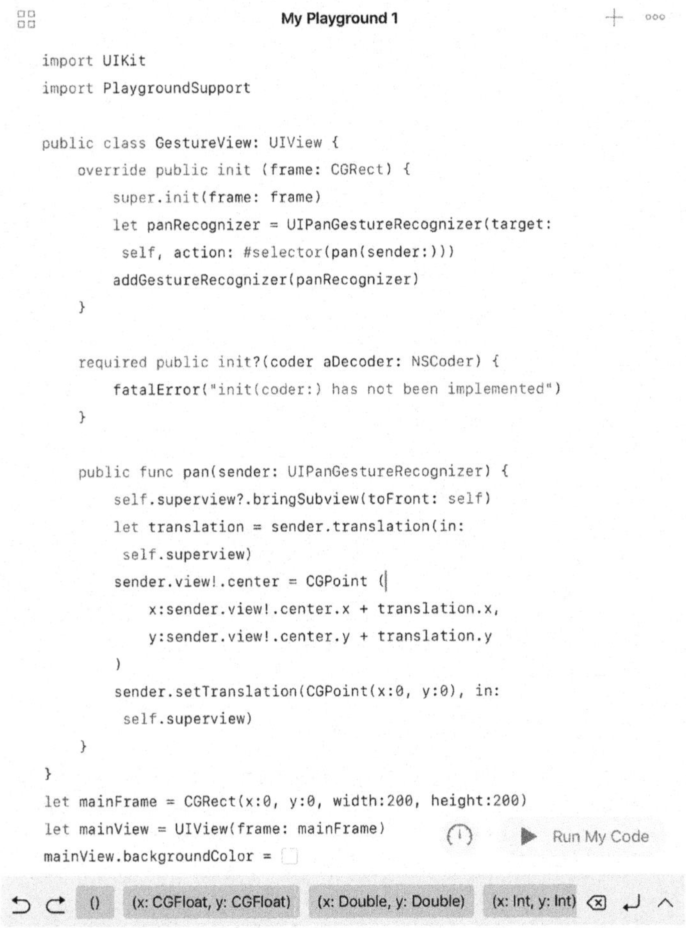

```
import UIKit
import PlaygroundSupport

public class GestureView: UIView {
    override public init (frame: CGRect) {
        super.init(frame: frame)
        let panRecognizer = UIPanGestureRecognizer(target:
         self, action: #selector(pan(sender:)))
        addGestureRecognizer(panRecognizer)
    }

    required public init?(coder aDecoder: NSCoder) {
        fatalError("init(coder:) has not been implemented")
    }

    public func pan(sender: UIPanGestureRecognizer) {
        self.superview?.bringSubview(toFront: self)
        let translation = sender.translation(in:
         self.superview)
        sender.view!.center = CGPoint (|
            x:sender.view!.center.x + translation.x,
            y:sender.view!.center.y + translation.y
        )
        sender.setTranslation(CGPoint(x:0, y:0), in:
         self.superview)
    }
}
let mainFrame = CGRect(x:0, y:0, width:200, height:200)
let mainView = UIView(frame: mainFrame)
mainView.backgroundColor = □
```

(⌒)   ▶ Run My Code

↺ ↻   ()   (x: CGFloat, y: CGFloat)   (x: Double, y: Double)   (x: Int, y: Int) ⊗ ↵ ⌃

Figure 8-11. *The entire playground in Playgrounds on iPad*

You can test it, as shown in Figure 8-12. It should work the same way as it does in Xcode on macOS.

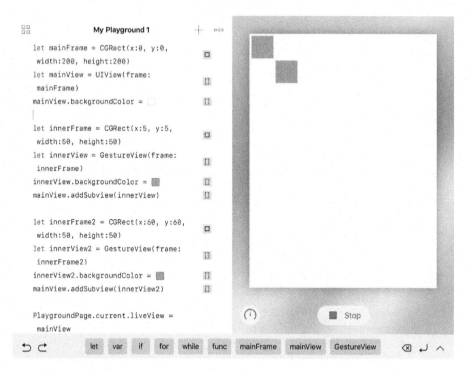

Figure 8-12. *Test the code on iPad*

As you're entering the code, if you type it you may notice that as you are about to set the background color (or, in fact any color in a playground), you'll be given a choice from the color palette, as shown in Figure 8-13.

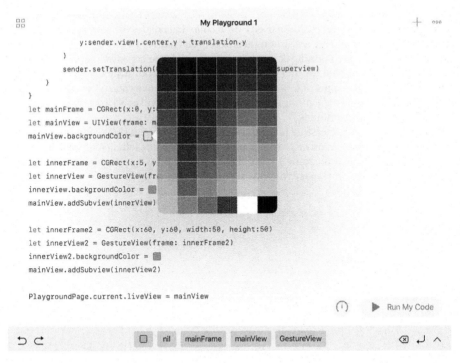

My Playground 1

```
        y:sender.view!.center.y + translation.y
    )
    sender.setTranslation(                    superview)
    }
}
let mainFrame = CGRect(x:0, y:
let mainView = UIView(frame: m
mainView.backgroundColor =

let innerFrame = CGRect(x:5, y
let innerView = GestureView(fr
innerView.backgroundColor =
mainView.addSubview(innerView)

let innerFrame2 = CGRect(x:60, y:60, width:50, height:50)
let innerView2 = GestureView(frame: innerFrame2)
innerView2.backgroundColor =
mainView.addSubview(innerView2)

PlaygroundPage.current.liveView = mainView
```

▶ Run My Code

nil   mainFrame   mainView   GestureView

Figure 8-13. *Set the color in Playgrounds on iPad*

Working with Gestures in a Playground

The previous sections of this chapter show you how to build a simple playground that incorporates gestures. As noted, it's a basic getting-started overview. In this section, you'll see how to restructure the playground into a more robust structure that you can then use for the basis of serious playground (and app) development.

Chapter 7 showed you how to add source code to a playground by putting it in the Sources folder so that the main playground can use it without your users getting into the weeds. The GestureView class is a great candidate for such a structure. This section shows you how to split a playground apart so that you move part of it into a Sources file.

■ **Note**   Splitting a playground apart like this is a bit easier to do with Xcode at this time, but once you've restructured your code (a matter of a minute or two if you follow the steps in this section), you can continue working on the playground either with Playgrounds on iPad or Xcode on your Mac.

BasicGesture is constructed so that the GestureView class is placed at the beginning of the playground so it can easily be used by the code that creates GestureView instances later in the playground. This is a structural choice: you could create an equally well-organized playground by putting GestureView at the end. You can also intermingle the code for GestureView with the other code in the playground, but structuring playgrounds and apps to keep the supporting structures apart from the active code is generally a good idea. (This an example of *factoring* or *decomposition*. If you will be writing much code, it is good to use these techniques.)

Begin from the BasicGesture playground from this chapter, as shown in Listing 8-8. (If you have created a version on Playgrounds for iPad, the color setting may look different, but underneath it will be the same.) Show the project navigator by using the button at the top right of the Xcode workspace window, as shown in Figure 8-14.

Project Navigator

Show Navigator

Figure 8-14. *Show the project navigator for the playground in Xcode on macOS*

At the bottom left, use the + to create a new file. Xcode shows you the files that it can create, as shown in Figure 8-15. Choose Swift File.

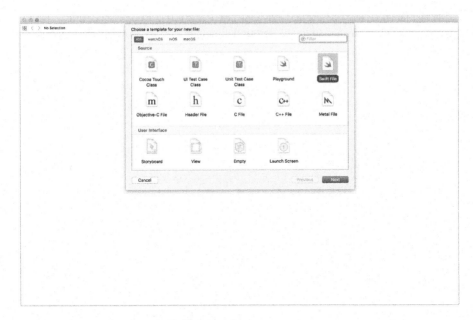

Figure 8-15. *Create a new Swift file in Xcode*

Click Next and then name and place the file. In Figure 8-16, you see it being named GestureSwiftClass (but you can name it anything), and it is placed in a local folder called Files. You can put it anywhere, because you'll be moving it.

Figure 8-16. *Name and place your Swift file*

Now that you have the new file, move the GestureView class code out of the playground and into the file. In the playground, highlight the GestureView class, as shown in Figure 8-17.

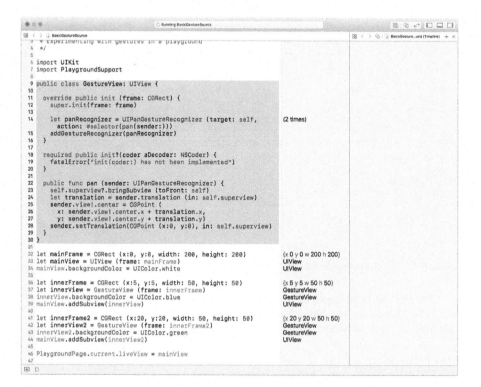

Figure 8-17. *Highlight the* GestureView *class code*

Cut the class definition (you will paste it into a Sources file shortly). When you cut the class definition, you will immediately generate some errors in the remaining code that refers to the now-cut class, as you see in Figure 8-18. Don't worry about the errors at this point.

Figure 8-18. *Don't worry about errors as you cut and paste code*

Paste the GestureView code that you just cut into the file you created in Figure 8-16 and save it. It should look like Figure 8-19, and the errors should be gone now that the GestureView class is defined in the Sources folder's GestureViewClass file.

Figure 8-19. *Paste the code in*

Return to the + at the bottom of the file navigator and this time choose Add Files to GesturePlayground (or whatever the name of your playground is). After you add the file, you'll see it in the file navigator in the Sources folder. (If necessary, the Sources folder will be created for you automatically.) Figure 8-20 shows the Add Files command as well as the structure that results in the file navigator after you have used it.

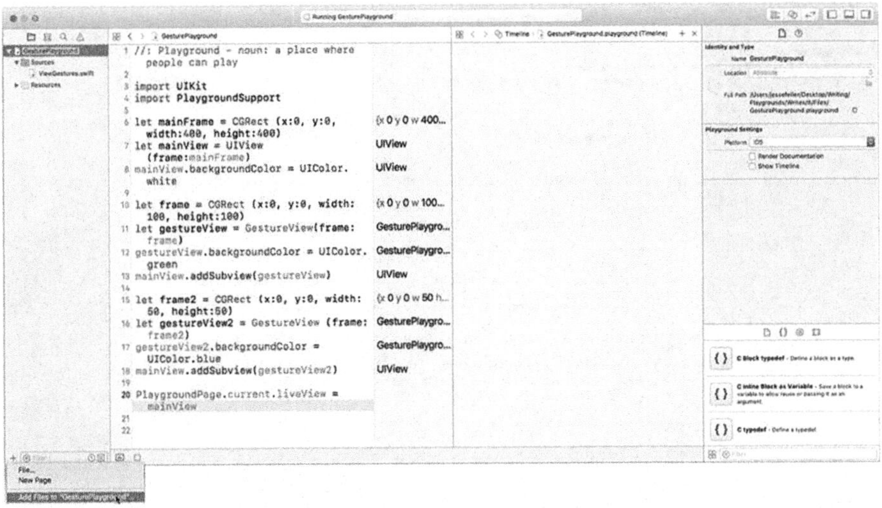

Figure 8-20.

You can now show the timeline, and you should be able to move the two shapes around, as you can see in Figures 8-21 and 8-22.

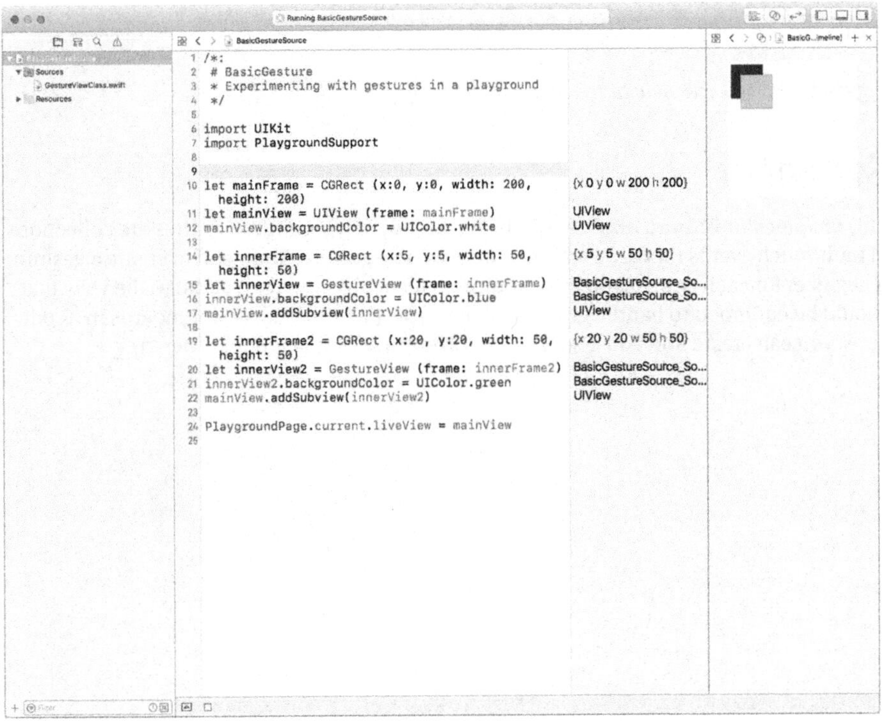

Figure 8-21. *Test the app*

Figure 8-22. *Move a view in the app to test the gesture*

Summary

This chapter showed you how to explore gestures in playgrounds. Gestures are collections of multitouch events that are combined into a single gesture. You need to create a gesture recognizer for each type of gesture you want to recognize and then add it to the view that should be equipped to handle gestures of that type. (When you use storyboards in Xcode apps, you can create and add gesture recognizers in a storyboard for a view.)

CHAPTER 9

■ ■ ■

Building a Complex Playground

The playgrounds you've seen in the other chapters of this book are one page long (*page* means a playground page and not necessarily a printed page). The heart of each playground page is the code that assigns the live view of the current page to a view or view controller that contains the playground page:

```
PlaygroundPage.current.liveView = your playground view
```

■ **Tip**   Remember that technically the current page can be any object that conforms to the `PlaygroundLiveViewable` protocol. Objects that conform to this protocol include `UIView`, `UIViewController`, `NSView`, and `NSViewController`. Subclasses of those objects that you create automatically conform to `PlaygroundLiveViewable`.

You can combine multiple pages into a playground easily using Xcode on macOS. (Becase this involves manipulating files, it's easier to do it on macOS than iOS, at least at the time of this writing.) As you do so in Xcode, basic navigation from page to page is automatically implemented. You can modify it or add your own to create a multi-page playground. This chapter shows you how to do build a multi-page playground and implement page-to-page navigation. You'll also see how to use playground links to navigate to web pages and any other web link resource.

Collecting Your Playground Pages and Creating the MultiPlayground

Begin by collecting a few playground pages—DataEntry and Interactive from Chapter 6 and GesturePlayground from Chapter 8. If you haven't worked on them, download them as described in the Introduction and put them somewhere safe so you can modify them easily.

© Jesse Feiler 2017

J. Feiler, *Exploring Swift Playgrounds*, DOI 10.1007/978-1-4842-2647-6_9

Start by creating a new playground (I call it MultiPlayground) that will combine the playgrounds you have collected. Figure 9-1 shows MultiPlayground started in Xcode.

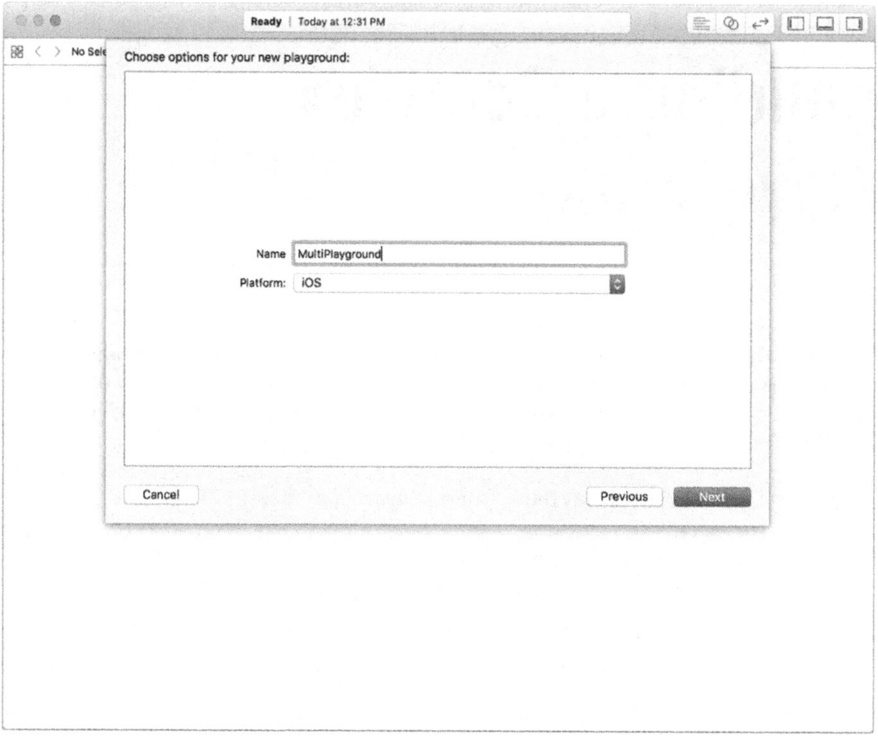

Figure 9-1. *Create the MultiPlayground playground*

After you have created the playground and stored it on disk, show the project navigator, as shown previously in Figure 8-14 in Chapter 8. Then click the menu in the lower left frame of the window to open the menu shown in Figure 9-2. (You may remember that you used this menu in Chapter 8 to add a file to your playground.) Rather than adding a file, use the New Page command to add a new page to the playground. Before you do so, take a moment to look at the structure of the playground.

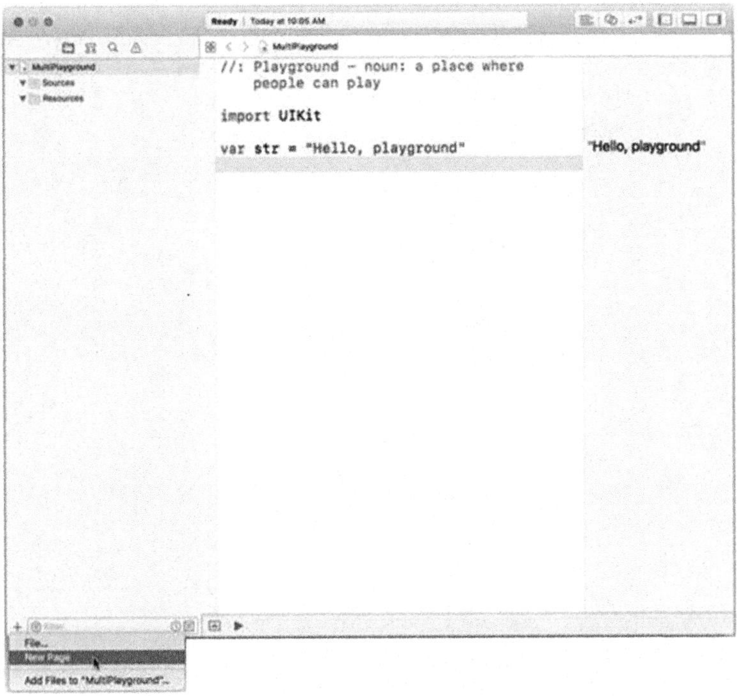

Figure 9-2. *Add a new page to the playground*

As you can see in Figure 9-2, the playground consists of the main playground page file, and within it are the Sources and Resources folders. (If they're not there yet, don't worry—they will be placed there when you need them.)

As soon as you release the mouse button (or lift your finger off the keypad), the New Page command will be executed, and you'll see the workspace changed so that it looks like Figure 9-3.

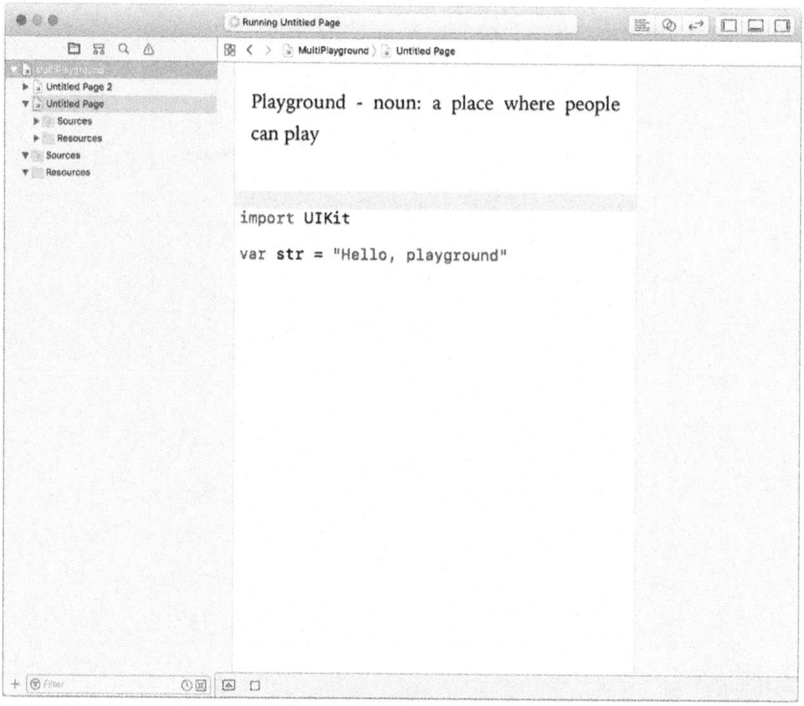

Figure 9-3. *View the result of adding a page to the playground*

Very quickly, the following things happen:

- A page named Untitled Page is created.

- A second page named Untitled Page 2 is created.

The project navigator may also be rearranged a little to accommodate the new files.
You may wonder why you have two files when you only asked for one. What actually
has happened is that the code from your original playground has been moved to Untitled
Page, and that's what you see in Figure 9-3.

■ **Note**   If you want to verify this, after you create the new playground, delete the template
code that you see in Figure 9-2 and replace it with a comment like this: `// My Comment`

You'll see that it has become Untitled Page. The original playground file contains the playground workspace and playground xcplayground file as well as a new Pages folder, shown in Figure 9-4 in the Finder when you show the package contents of the `MultiPlayground.playground` file.

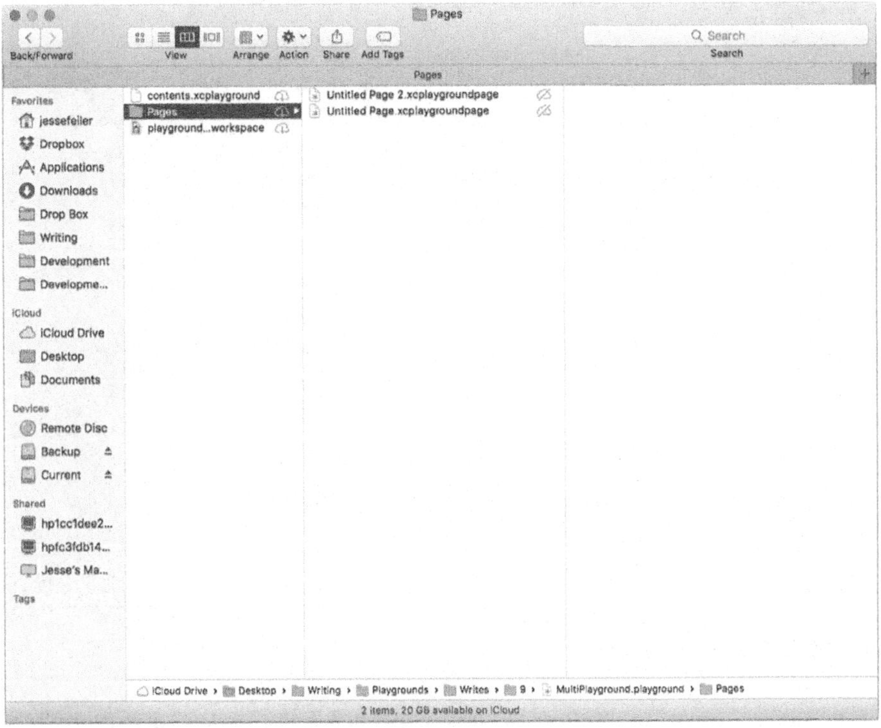

Figure 9-4. *Look inside the playground package*

If you open the folders in the new playground, as shown in Figure 9-5, you'll see that each playground page has its own Sources and Resources folders.

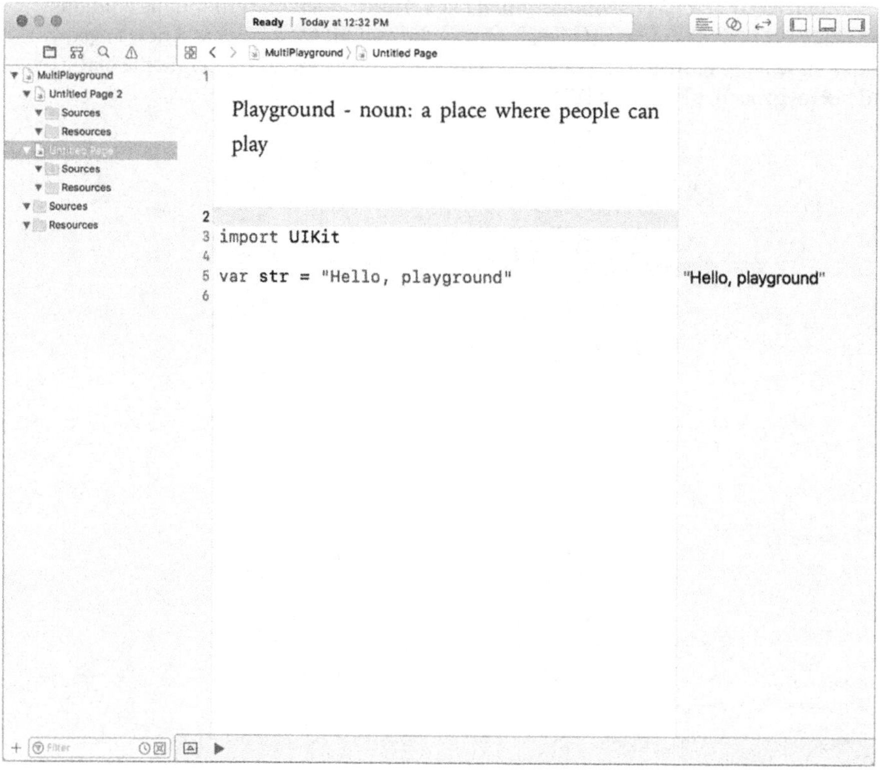

Figure 9-5. *Look inside a page*

In addition, you'll see a Sources and Resources folder at the top level of the playground page. It may not be immediately apparent in Figure 9-5, but if you look at the left margins of the Untitled Page 2 and Untitled Page, you'll see that they align with the Sources and Resources folders for the playground as a whole (the bottom two folders in Figure 9-5.

Assembling Playground Pages for Basic Navigation

You can move from one playground page to another by clicking it in the project navigator. Remember, typically Untitled Page will be the playground page you started from; it's copied into the multi-file playground. You can drag the pages to another order if you want, but remember not to move the Sources and Resources folders out of a page because they may be needed to support that page.

Untitled Page 2 is a brand new page that has been created by the New Page command that you executed (refer to Figure 9-2 as a reminder). The rendered version of Untitled Page 2 is shown in Figure 9-6, and you can see that it has Next/Previous navigation added to it.

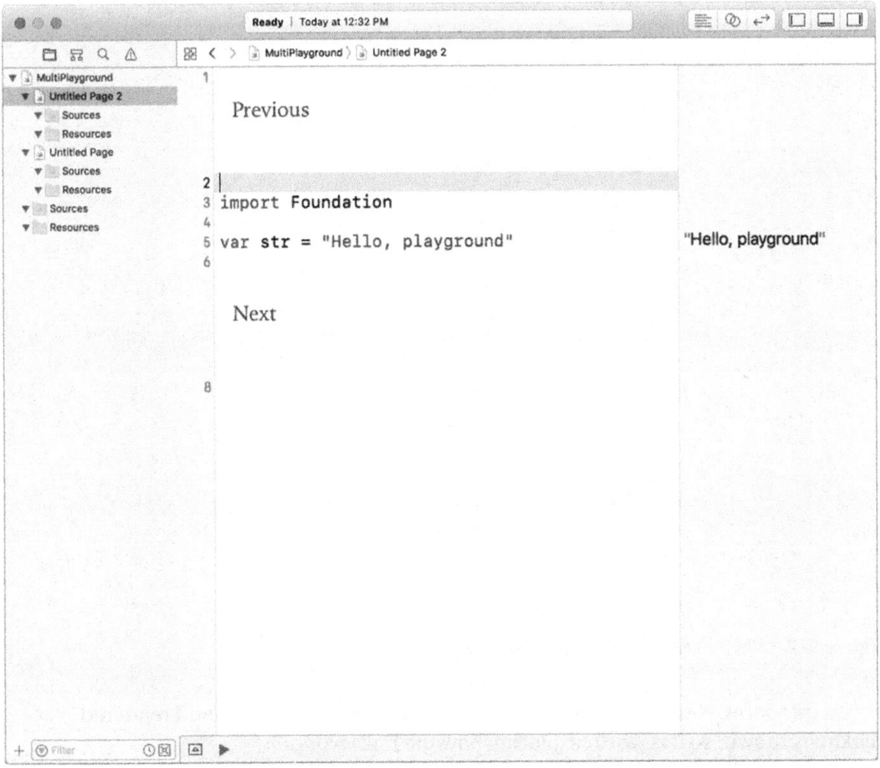

Figure 9-6. *Next/Previous rendered markup added automatically to a new page*

Figure 9-7 shows the raw markup.

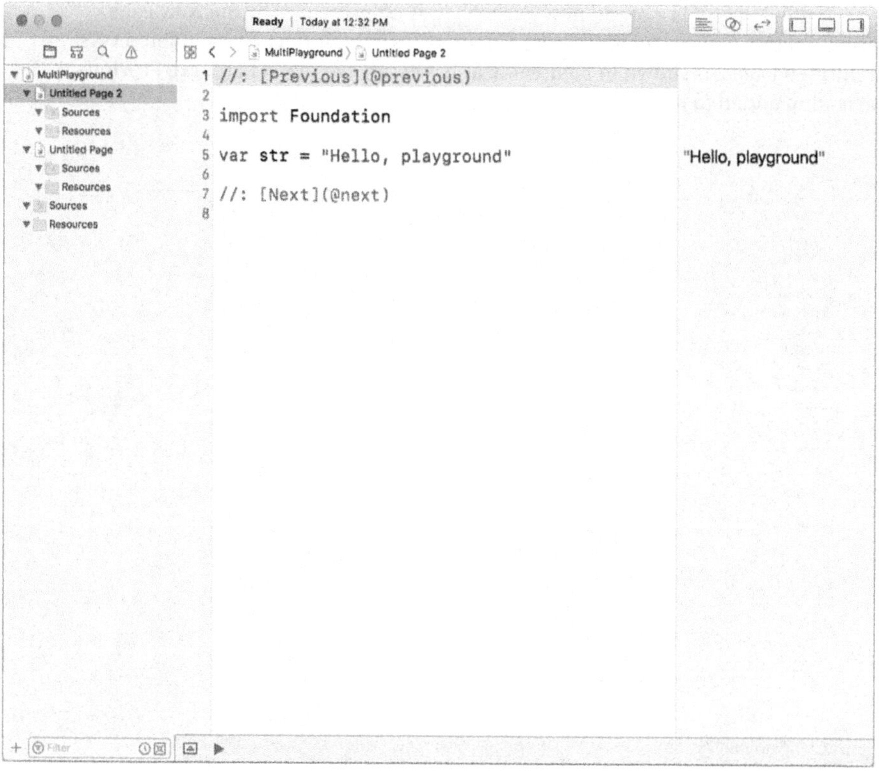

Figure 9-7. *Next/Previous raw markup code*

At this point, Next should work when Untitled Page 2 is selected and rendered markup is shown, so it is worth exploring how the links work.

Using Basic Link Navigation

Basic Next/Previous links rely on the project navigator and the sequence of files it contains. Remember that each file can be expanded to show its subfolders (Sources and Resources). In Figure 9-8 the files have been closed up so the subfolders aren't visible. This makes it possible to click in a file name and start to edit it, as you see in Figure 9-8.

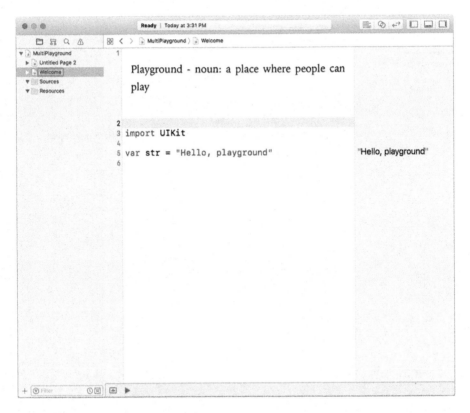

Figure 9-8. *Rename a page in the project navigator*

Untitled Page 2 should have the Next and Previous links (as you see in Figure 9-9).

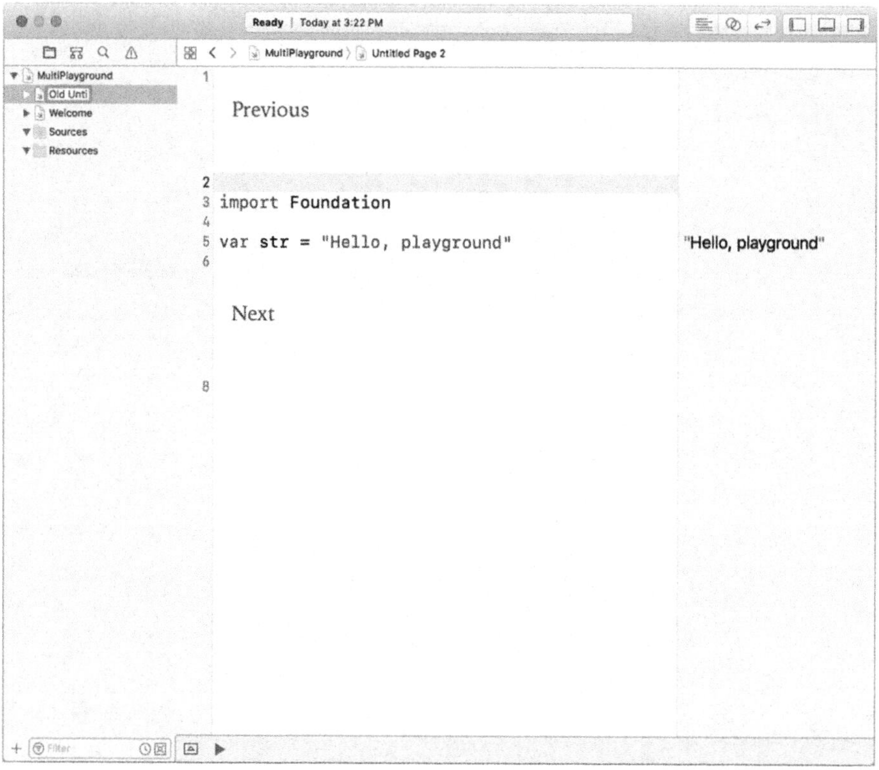

Figure 9-9. *Double-check Next/Previous rendered markup in a renamed page*

If you're curious, you can try them out. You'll see that Previous doesn't work, but Next takes you to the Welcome page, as you can see in Figure 9-10.

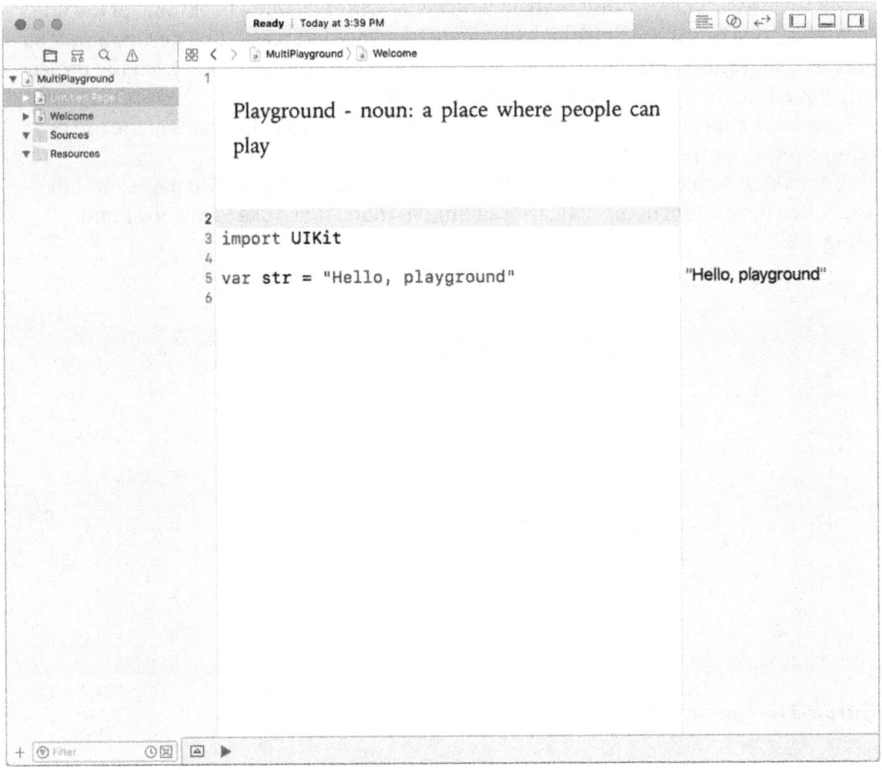

Figure 9-10. Click Next in Untitled Page 2 and go to the Welcome page

Next and Previous links rely on the order of pages in the project navigator. At this point, the order is as follows:

- Untitled Page 2

- Welcome

Reverse the seqeuence by dragging the files in the project navigator so that Welcome is the first page and you'll be ready to continue. You've seen the Next/Previous code in Figures 9-6 and 9-7. Figure 9-7 is the more complete version; its code is shown in Listing 9-1.

Listing 9-1. Code for Next/Previous links

```
//: [Previous](@previous)

import Foundation

var str = "Hello, playground"

//: [Next](@next)
```

As always with playground markup, you begin with //: at the beginning of the line. The format for a link is the link name in square brackets and then a link destination. The @previous and @next link destinations are generated by the playground from the project navigator based on the position of the current page.

The links appear where you want them to on a page. Typically, that's at the top or bottom, as is the case with this code.

To make your playground work properly, you can add links to both pages. Add the Next link to the bottom of the code in Welcome so that it looks like Figure 9-11 and Listing 9-2.

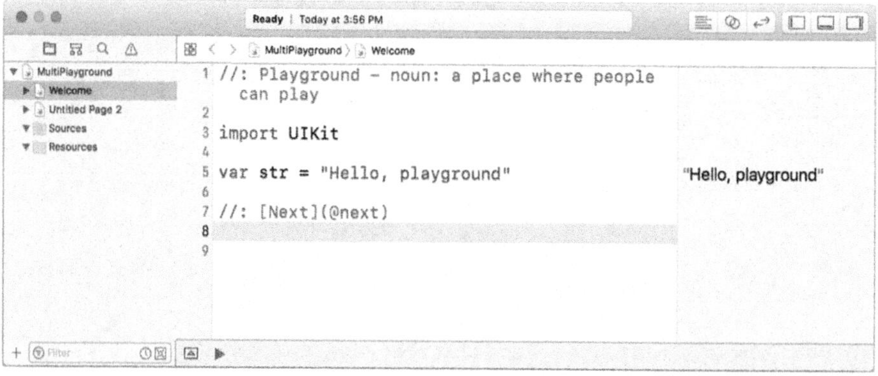

Figure 9-11. *Add Next to Welcome*

Listing 9-2. Code for Next (no Previous) navigation

```
//: Playground - noun: a place where people can play

import UIKit

var str = "Hello, playground"

//: [Next](@next)
```

You can bring Untitled Page 2 up to date by going to the existing code, shown in Figure 9-12.

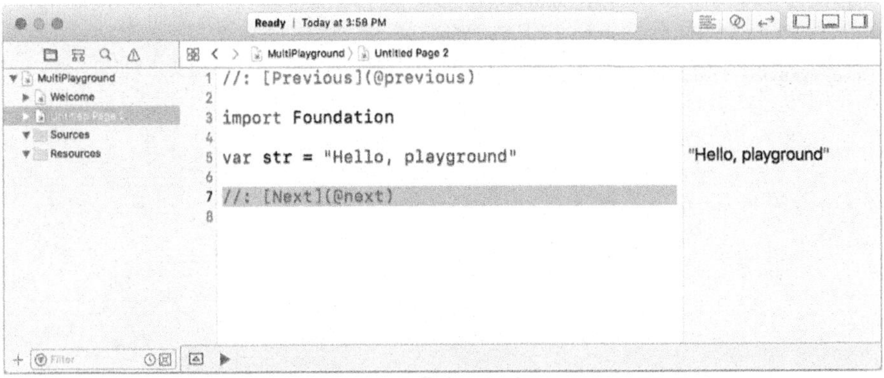

Figure 9-12. *Next/Previous links on a new middle page*

This is the new page that was added to your basic playground. As a new page, it can serve as a model for all your pages: it is a middle page, so it has both Next and Previous links on it. For now, you can remove the Next link because there is no next page in the project navigator. Your code should look like Listing 9-3 at this point.

Listing 9-3. Remove the Next Link from a Final Page

```
//: [Previous](@previous)

import Foundation

var str = "Hello, playground"
```

You can open the playground, show the rendered markup, and run it with the Next and Previous buttons. You can even hide the project navigator so your playground is self-contained.

You can move it to your iPad and run it, as shown in Figures 9-13 and 9-14.

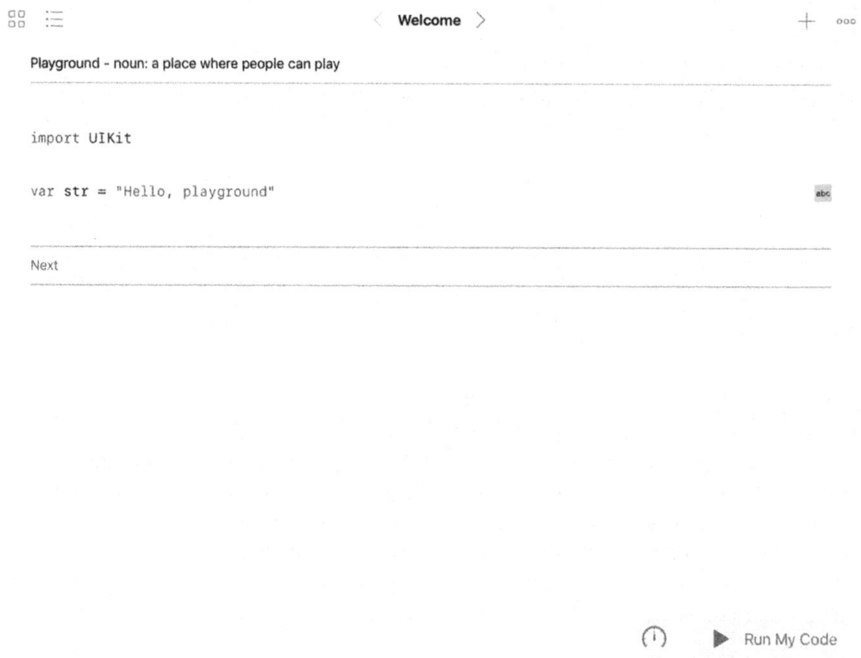

⬚⬚ ☰   ‹ **Welcome** ›   + ᵒᵒᵒ

Playground - noun: a place where people can play

```
import UIKit

var str = "Hello, playground"
```

Next

⟲   ▶ Run My Code

Figure 9-13. *Welcome page with a Next link*

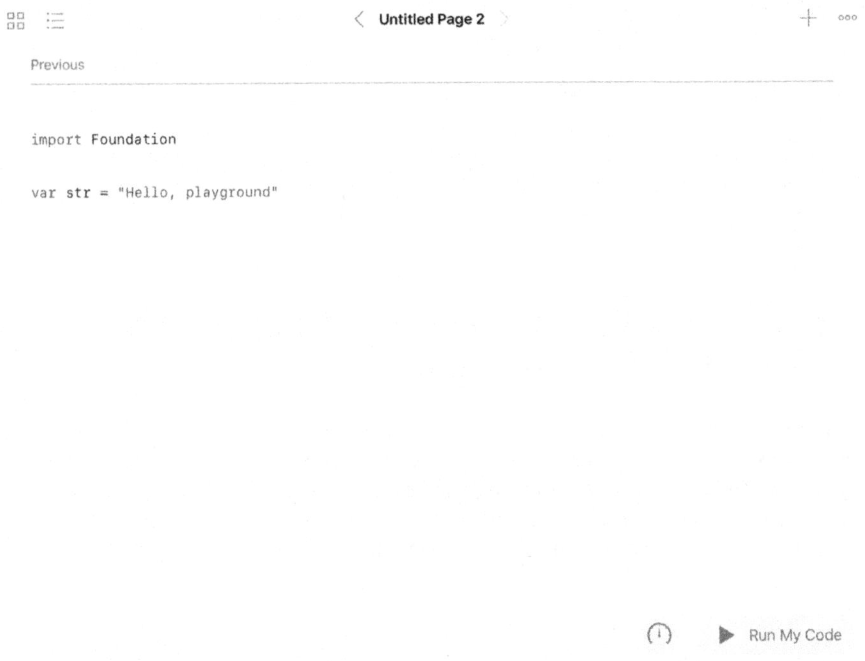

⊞ ☰   ‹ **Untitled Page 2** ›   + ∘∘∘

Previous
_____

```
import Foundation

var str = "Hello, playground"
```

⊙   ▶ Run My Code

Figure 9-14. *Middle page with a Previous link*

Enhancing Navigation

There are many things you can do to improve the navigation in this playground. You may want to use some of them in other playgrounds—sometimes as a standard practice.

Changing Link and File Names

Cleaning up your MultiPlayground now is a good idea: rename files as necessary and change the links to match. Renaming files as soon as possible is a good idea. When you come back to MultiPlayground after a weekend, you may not remember what Untitled Page 2 was.

Renaming a file in the project navigator is very simple: you click in the file name and type the new one. For the moment, it can make sense to rename Untitled Page 2 to be Middle Page. (You will shortly remove it entirely from the playground.) Figure 9-15 shows the renamed file in the project navigator.

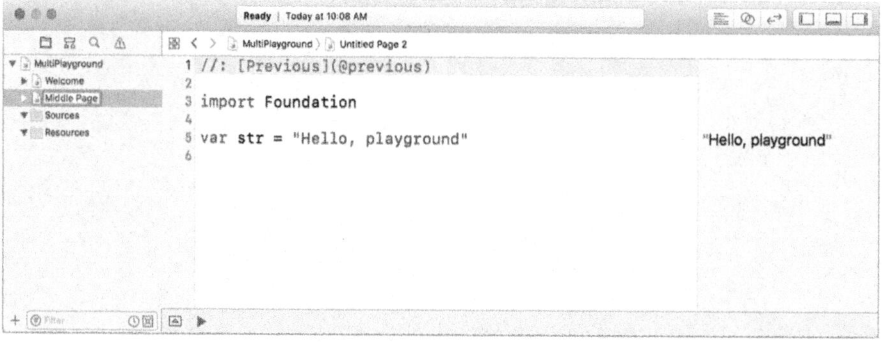

Figure 9-15. *Rename a file in the project naviagator*

The playground works as it has in the past because the Next and Previous links go to the next and previous pages relative to the current page in the project navigator. Playgrounds on your iPad shows the name of each page along with Next/Previous arrows at the top of each page. As you see in Figure 9-16, Middle Page is now named appropriately, and the navigation still works even though you have renamed the files.

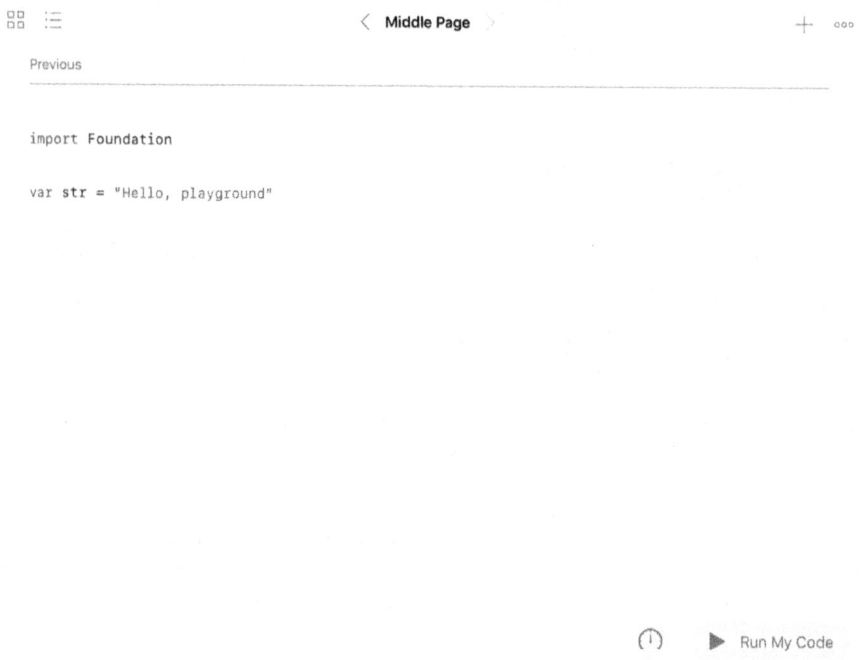

Figure 9-16. *On Playgrounds for iPad, renamed pages have appropriate arrows shown (or not)*

This doesn't mean that you don't break links when you rename a page in a playground; you just don't break the Next/Previous links. (And you do break them if you rearrange the files; you'll always go to the next or previous page relative to the current page in the project navigator).

Adding a Constant Link (Home)

You sometimes do want to add a link to a specific page rather than the Next/Previous page. A common such link is a link to the first page in a playground. In MultiPlayground at the moment, that file is named Welcome. It happens to be the previous page from Middle Page at the moment, but if you had more pages, you still may want to go back to it from wherever you are.

The syntax for a constant link is similar to the links you've already seen. It starts with the text to be displayed in square brackets and then has the page to link to in parentheses. Thus, the link to Welcome will look like this:

```
//: [Welcome](Welcome)
```

You can see it in raw markup in Figure 9-17 and in rendered markup in Figure 9-18.

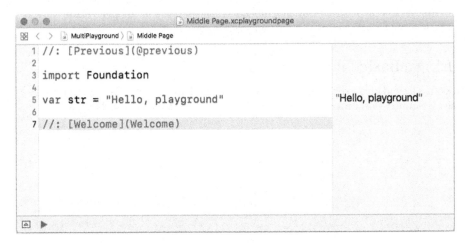

Figure 9-17. *Raw markup for named links*

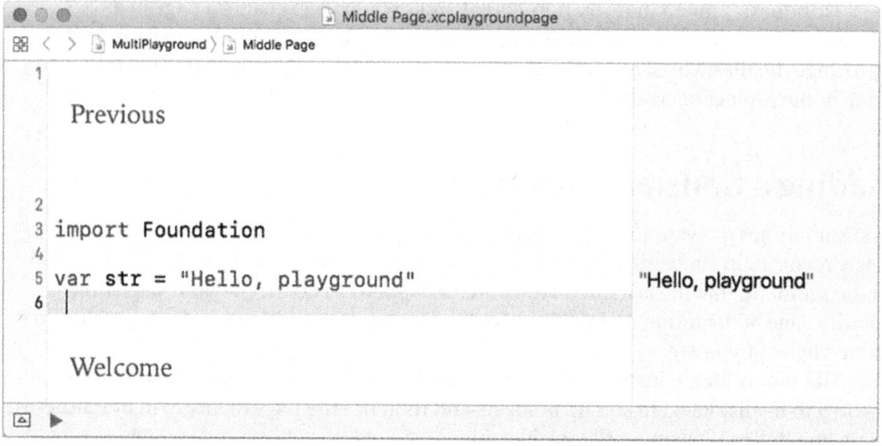

Figure 9-18. *Rendered markup for named links*

It's important to note that neither the link name in square brackets or the page name in parentheses is enclosed in quotes. Note too that although the link name can be anything you want, the page name is case-sensitive. Also note that the page name in the parentheses is a single string with no embedded spaces. If you have a page name with an embedded space, you have to use the escape code you would use in a URL: %20.

Using a Basic File for All Pages

It's often a good idea to have a standard section of markup on each of your playground pages. Figure 9-19 shows what the raw code for Welcome can look in such cases.

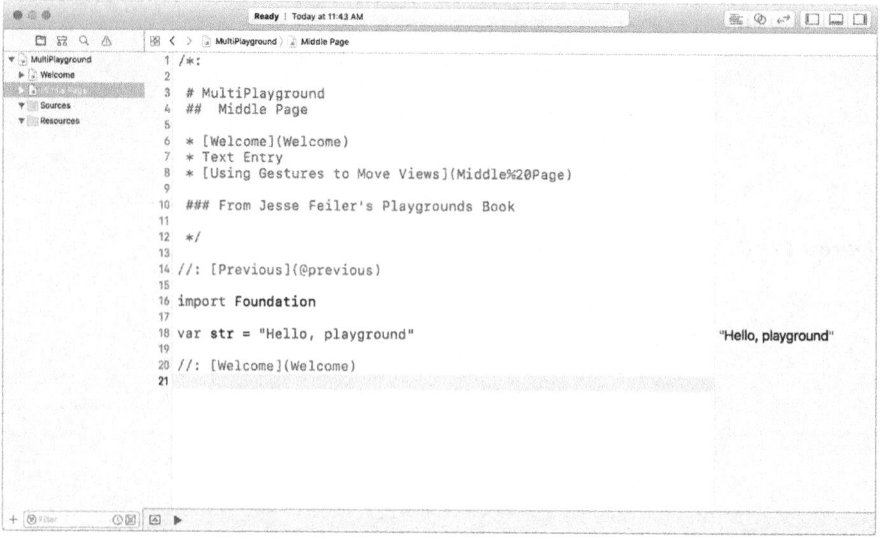

Figure 9-19. *Basic code for a middle page*

Figure 9-20 shows Welcome rendered.

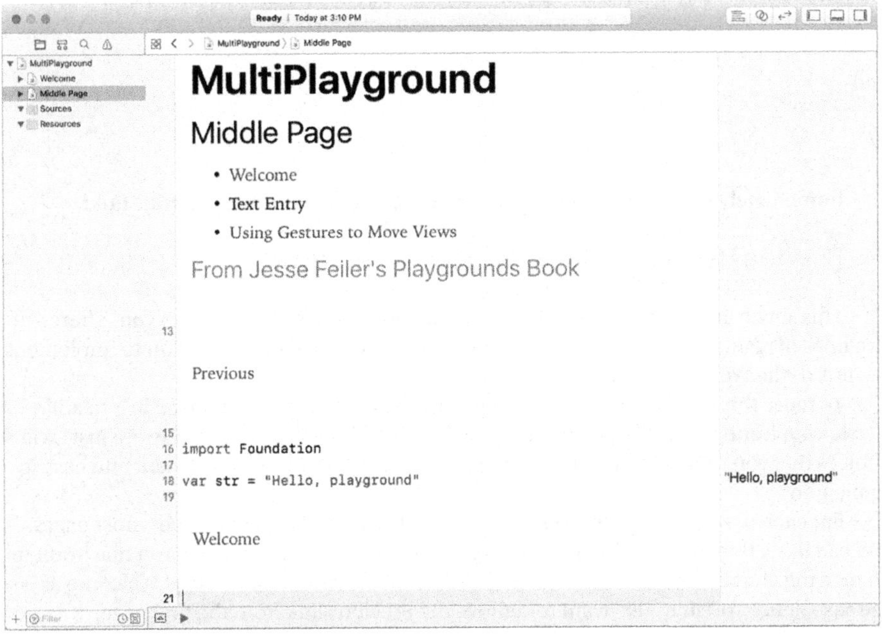

Figure 9-20. *Rendered markup for Welcome*

The code itself is shown in Listing 9-4.

Listing 9-4. Standard Page Raw Markup for a Playground

```
/*:

# MultiPlayground
## Middle Page

* [Welcome](Welcome)
* Text Entry
* [Using Gestures to Move Views](Middle%20Page)

### From Jesse Feiler's Playgrounds Book

*/

//: [Previous](@previous)

import Foundation

var str = "Hello, playground"

//: [Welcome](Welcome)
```

185

As you create playgrounds, having some consistency can make your job easier; it also makes it easier for users of your playground. The entire section of code is enclosed in

```
/*:
```

and

```
*/
```

Immediately following, a single line of markup implements the Previous link:

```
//: [Previous]*(@previous)
```

This single line could be added to the main block, but it's totally up to you. There are two lines of regular playground code, and then there's a final line of markup to implement the link to the Welcome page.

To reuse this code, one strategy is to place the name of the playground in a headline 1 style with # and the name of the specific page in headline 2 with ##. These are just style choices that you may want to use. What's important is that they be consistent and easy to implement.

For each playground page, you just need to change the page name. For most pages, you can use a Previous and Next link without making any other changes. You may want to change the Next link on the last page to the name of the first page (such as Welcome as is the case here). You may also want to remove the Previous link from the first page.

■ **Tip** If you make changes like this, remember to redo them if you rearrange the pages in your playground.

Making Further Enhancements

In Chapter 8 you saw how to create the GestureView class, which can be used to move views around with multitouch gestures. At the end of the chapter, GestureView is moved to be in its own file in the Sources folder of the playground page.

A class like this might be useful for more than one playground; in that case, you can move it to the Sources folder for the entire playground rather than sources for a single playground page. Keep an eye out for classes such as this one that can be used to build your own library of playground classes. (That's also a good way to learn how to structure apps!)

Summary

In this chapter you saw how to start adding new pages to a playground and how to implement links based on the names of pages in the project navigator as well as their relative positions. Expand your playgrounds with code that's hidden on pages or places in files in the Sources folder for a specific page or for the playground as a whole.

What you create with Swift playgrounds is up to you—the possibilities are literally endless. You can use playgrounds to test your own code snippets as you're building apps or other playgrounds, or you can use Swift playgrounds as the framework for implementing documentation, teaching, or training materials.

The code that you write in playgrounds is transportable to apps that you write (the playground markup will be passed over as comments when pasted into apps).

When you're thinking about building a playground, you need to think about what you want to accomplish with it, and in particular how the code needs to work. Whether you want to focus on writing control code that manipulates functionalities defined in Sources or you want to do the reverse and focus on writing the functional code that control structures in Sources will use, Swift playgrounds can not only make your job easier but help you to define it more precisely.

Index

© Jesse Feiler 2017
J. Feiler, *Exploring Swift Playgrounds*, DOI 10.1007/978-1-4842-2647-6

■ T, U, V, W

■ X, Y, Z

Get the eBook for only $5!

Why limit yourself?

With most of our titles available in both PDF and ePUB format, you can access your content wherever and however you wish—on your PC, phone, tablet, or reader.

Since you've purchased this print book, we are happy to offer you the eBook for just $5.

To learn more, go to http://www.apress.com/companion or contact support@apress.com.

Apress®

CPSIA information can be obtained
at www.ICGtesting.com
Printed in the USA
LVOW04s1040180517
534996LV00012B/260/P